Writings On Canadian English 1792-1975

An Annotated Bibliography

Walter S. Avis
A. M. Kinloch

Fitzhenry & Whiteside
Toronto Montreal Winnipeg Vancouver

This book was photo-offset from an original typed on an IBM Correcting "Selectric" typewriter, using a Delegate 10 Pitch element, supplemented by a Camwil Part No. 113M (phonetic symbol) element. This book was produced under the direction of Mr. Dennis Bockus, with the aid of Mrs. Joanne Barchard, Miss Jane Ryley, and Mr. Ian Gillen.

Fitzhenry & Whiteside Limited
953 Dillingham Road
Pickering, Ontario
L1W 1Z7

Canadian Cataloguing in Publication Data

Avis, Walter Spencer
Writings on Canadian English, 1792-1975: an annotated bibliography

ISBN: 0-88902-121-X clothbound
0-88902-120-1 paperbound

1. English language in Canada--Bibliography
I. Kinloch, A. Murray jt. author
II. Title

Z 1379 016.427'971

Printed in Canada

PREFACE

Scholarship on Canadian English

The forerunner of this present book, A Bibliography of Writings on Canadian English (1857-1965) by Walter S. Avis, listed 168 titles; it is itself item 103 in this work, which records 723 titles, including those in the Addendum. Several factors have contributed to this increase in size. The authors of this work decided to push the beginning date back to 1792; they thus include the "Glossary" in the Journal of Transactions and Events During a Residence of Nearly Sixteen Years on the Coast of Labrador by George Cartwright, item 192. In so doing, they incidentally displace Rev. A. Constable Geikie from the position he has long held, through his authorship of item 289, as the earliest writer on Canadian English. The years which have elapsed since the publication of Avis's bibliography have been extremely rich in scholarship on Canadian English. This period saw more than a decade of lexicographical work in Canada crowned by the publication of the Dictionary of Canadianisms on Historical Principles, item 149, whose impact on the press produced many reviews. It saw more of the American scholarship on the communities along the Canada-United States border appear in print, e.g., item 012. It saw a major increase of interest in Canadian English in Canada itself, as is evidenced by the Survey of Canadian English and the works it produced, e.g., item 529, and by the fact that no less than four books on Canadian English have appeared since 1970, these being items 202, 484, 556, and 704. Finally, Canadian English has become a truly international study; the scholar who will read in the original all that is written of it must have access to English, French, German, and Russian.

The sources of this work

There is not now, and there never has been, any one publication that lists annually everything written on Canadian English. The compiler of a bibliography on this topic must search through dozens of indexes, etc., devoted to many different ends. For the benefit of future revisers of this present work, a list of the sources consulted in preparing it has been drawn up. This list is entitled "Sources of an Annotated Bibliography of Writings on Canadian English to 1975," and it will be lodged in the Harriet Irving Library of the University of New Brunswick.

The scope of this work

Certain matters have been deliberately excluded. Works on onomastics have been omitted, except for those that convey other information as well, e.g., item 568. So, too, technical glossaries have been left out unless they give information on some aspect of Canadian English beyond their particular fields. Works dealing with the influence of Canadian English on other languages, notably French and Malecite, have likewise been excluded. Pedagogical and prescriptive works do not appear in this bibliography; thus, manuals of style have been ignored as dealing with what should be, or with what someone thinks should be, and not with what actually is. In the matter of scope, where decision was difficult, the authors decided to err on the side of liberality and to include any work in question.

Articles on the history of the Canadian Linguistic Association have been included. This association has done much to further an interest in Canadian English and, so far as the authors are aware, these articles are nowhere else listed.

Within these limits, the authors have striven hard for complete coverage of relevant items up to December 31, 1975; no doubt, they have failed to achieve this. Even after this work had been put in its final form, several bibliographies for 1975 still had not appeared. The authors received their copies of the 1975 MLA International Bibliography only during the very last stages of the preparation of the manuscript.

The arrangement of this work: Bibliography and Addendum

The main bibliography contains entries for

> all works published before December 31, 1975, which were known to the authors;
>
> all multi-volume works whose first volume appeared before December 31, 1975;
>
> works first published before December 31, 1975, and reprinted verbatim during 1976 or 1977.

The Addendum contains entries for

> some works published before December 31, 1975, but obtained too late for inclusion in the main bibliography. For ease of identification, these have been starred (*) in the Addendum;
>
> the more important works published during 1976 and the first six months of 1977;
>
> some other works published during 1976 and 1977 that have come to the authors' notice.

The annotations

The authors have tried not to obtrude their own theoretical prejudices into the annotations; these latter are mainly the work of A.M. Kinloch, who must bear the total responsibility for errors and faults therein.

Acknowledgments

The authors were privileged to see a pre-publication copy of the bibliography from Dr. Ruth McConnell's forthcoming book on Canadian English. To mention all those who answered the annotator's letters and telephone calls would make a very long list indeed. However, the authors feel they must acknowledge the help they received from: Mr. P.D. Drysdale, Professors R.J. Gregg, John Orrell, Harold J. Paddock, G.M. Story, M.G. Wanamaker, H.J. Warkentyne, Reginald Eyre Watters, and H. Rex Wilson; Mrs. T. Weiner, and, last but not least, Mrs. A.M. Kinloch, who most patiently read the proof.

Appeal to the reader

Should any reader know of relevant items that do not appear in this bibliography, he will perform a great service by sending the required bibliographical details to either of the authors or to the publisher for inclusion in subsequent revisions.

C O N T E N T S

LIST OF ABBREVIATIONS

AA — *American Anthropologist.*

AE — American English.

AfrLRev — *African Language Review.*

AS — *American Speech.*

BD — *The Beginning Dictionary.* See item 152.

BE — British English.

CAB — *Canadian Author and Bookman.*

CanL — *Canadian Literature.*

CDC — *A Concise Dictionary of Canadianisms.* See item 148.

CE — Canadian English.

CJL — *Canadian Journal of Linguistics.* Up to and including 6:3 (Spring 1961), this is *JCLA*, q.v.

CLA — (The) Canadian Linguistic Association.

CTD — *The Canadian Teaching Dictionary for Junior Grades.* See item 449.

CWPL — *Calgary Working Papers in Linguistics.* LOGOS. Dept. of Linguistics, Univ. of Calgary.

DA — *A Dictionary of Americanisms on Historical Principles.* Ed. Mitford M. Mathews. 2 vols. (Chicago: Univ. of Chicago, 1951).

DAE — *Dictionary of American English.* Ed. W.A. Craigie and J.W. Hulbert. 4 vols. (Chicago: Univ. of Chicago, 1938-44).

DAI A — *Dissertation Abstracts International. Section A.*

DCCD — *Dictionnaire Canadien/The Canadian Dictionary.* See item 621.

DCE — (The) Dictionary of Canadian English.

DCHP — *A Dictionary of Canadianisms on Historical Principles*. See item 149.

DN — *Dialect Notes*.

DR — *Dalhousie Review*.

EE — *English Exchange*. Journal of the Ontario Council of Teachers of English.

ELN — *English Language Notes*.

EngQ — *English Quarterly*.

ERIC — Educational Resources Information Center.

FoLi — *Folia Linguistica*.

GCE — General Canadian English.

ID — *The Intermediate Dictionary*. See item 153.

JAF — *Journal of American Folklore*.

JAS — *Journal of the Acoustical Society*.

JCLA — *Journal of the Canadian Linguistic Association*. From and including 7:1 (Fall 1961), this is *CJL*, q.v.

JEGP — *Journal of English and Germanic Philology*.

JEngL — *Journal of English Linguistics*.

JSHR — *Journal of Speech and Hearing Research*.

L&S — *Language and Speech*.

LAUSC — (The) Linguistic Atlas of the United States and Canada.

LJ — *Library Journal*.

LSp — *Lebende Sprachen*.

ME — Middle English.

MLR — *Modern Language Review*.

NADS — *Newsletter of the American Dialect Society*.

NAE — North American English.

N&Q — *Notes and Queries*.

NS — *Die Neueren Sprachen*.

NYFQ	*New York Folklore Quarterly*.
OED	*The Oxford English Dictionary*.
PADS	*Publication of the American Dialect Society*.
PLCMND	*Proceedings of the Linguistic Circle of Manitoba and North Dakota*.
PTRSC	*Proceedings and Transactions of the Royal Society of Canada*.
QJS	*Quarterly Journal of Speech*.
QQ	*Queen's Quarterly*.
RLS	*Regional Language Studies ... Newfoundland*.
RSE	Received Standard English.
SatN	*Saturday Night*.
SCE	(The) Survey of Canadian English. See item 563.
SD	*The Senior Dictionary*. See item 151.
TLS	*The Times Literary Supplement*.
WI	*The Winston Dictionary of Canadian English*. Intermediate Edition. See item 492.
ZDL	*Zeitschrift für Dialektologie und Linguistik*.

B I B L I O G R A P H Y

001. A., A. "Sepper tizzum." *SatN*, Dec. 1973, p. 41-42.

This review of *Canajan, Eh?* by Mark M. Orkin, q.v., cites 11 of Orkin's examples but denies that Canadians say "Moundie" or "twendy." It asserts that some of Orkin's Canadianisms are merely the result of rapid enunciation. CE is said to be NAE with regional variations.

002. Ahrend, Evelyn R. "Ontario Speech." *AS*, 9 (1934), 136-39.

This article comments on the speech of Canadians from Kingston to Toronto. It mentions Canadian "raising " and the use of American slang and of occasional Briticisms. It specifies 8 features of pronunciation and gives a phonetic transcription of one informant's version of "Arthur the Rat."

003. Alexander, Henry. "Charting Canadian Speech." *Journal of Education* (Nova Scotia), 10 (1939), 457-58.

The author appeals for help with his linguistic survey of Nova Scotia. He shows why Nova Scotia is to be a starting point for Canada, outlines the methods to be used, and notes what such a survey will add to knowledge in general.

004. __________. "Collecting Canadian Speech." *Queen's Review*, 15 (1941), 45-47.

The author gives the object of his survey and the causes of the speech differences it aims to record. He then tells of some amusing experiences he had while doing fieldwork and comments on the usefulness of his survey.

005. __________. "The English Language in Canada," in *Royal Commission Studies*. Ottawa: King's Printer, 1951. p. 13-24.

The author claims that CE is closer to AE than to BE, since it lacks a prestige dialect, uses "flat-a," and pronounces /r/; also, it articulates unstressed syllables with care. He discusses the Canadian pronunciation of /t/. Morphologically and

Alexander, Henry. Cont'd.

lexically, CE again approximates AE. In spelling, CE uses both the American system and the British.

006. __________. "Is There a Canadian Language?" CBC Times, 27 Feb.-5 Mar. 1955, p. 2-3.

The author comments on the "more or less uniform type of English heard at the educated level." Similarities between CE and NAE show that there is "no exclusively Canadian form of English."

007. __________. "Linguistic Geography." QQ, 47 (1940), 38-47.

The author explains why fieldwork in Canada started in Nova Scotia and describes its methods. He exemplifies the influence of non-English languages, the adoption of technical terms into the everyday language, the survival of older usages, regional lexical variations, and semantic phenomena. Arguing hence, he questions some common assumptions on language.

008. __________. Review of A Dictionary of Canadianisms on Historical Principles, Walter S. Avis, Ed.-in-Chief. Weekend Magazine, 30 Dec. 1967, p. 13.

This review specifies the elements of Canadian life that seem to have contributed most to the Canadian lexicon. It notes Canadian lexical borrowing and commends DCHP's modernity.

009. __________. The Story of Our Language. Toronto: Thomas Nelson and Sons, 1940.

This book comments passim on CE. It notes the possibility that differences in early Germanic dialects have influenced CE and sees the English of central and western Canada as a branch of AE. It describes 5 phonological features, 16 words, and 1 idiom, most from Nova Scotia.

010. Allen, Harold B. "Canadian-American Differences Along the Middle Border," in Canadian English: Origins and Structures. Ed. J.K. Chambers (q.v.). p. 102-08.

This is a reprint of "Canadian-American Speech Differences Along the Middle Border" by Harold B. Allen, q.v.

Allen, Harold B. Cont'd.

011. ________. "Canadian-American Speech Differences Along the Middle Border." JCLA, 5 (1959), 17-24.

This study examines how far the "middle border" is a language barrier between AE and CE. The study is based on data from 5 communities, specified in item 012. It shows as exclusively Canadian 12 lexical items, the interrogative eh? and 6 phonological features. More typically Canadian than American are 16 lexical items, 1 syntactical item, and 4 phonological features. By contrast, 13 lexical items are exclusively American. The article concludes that the speech of Canadians is more distinctly Canadian than that of Americans is American and that American has had more influence on Canadian than vice versa.

012. ________. The Linguistic Atlas of the Upper Midwest. In 2 [later replanned to 3] vols. Minneapolis: Univ. of Minnesota, 1973-1976.

Volume 1 gives a detailed description of the project behind this work, including the methods of collecting, recording, and processing the data. Among the communities investigated were 5 from Canada: Sprague, Man., Fort Francis, Ont., Fort William, Ont., Estevan, Sask., and Killarney, Man., communities 1, 2, 3, 201, and 202 respectively. The numbers of responses obtained and discussed for each community are:

	1	2	3	201	202
lexis	304	304	304	325	325
morphology/syntax	107	103	107	110	100
phonology (vowels)	114	112	114	114	112

These data occupy volumes 1 and 2. In volume 3, the diaphones of each phoneme are described. A schematic table gives a synopsis of the stressed vowels of selected key words for each informant. Information on the consonants is given passim under the descriptions of seven different linguistic processes.

013. ________. "Pejorative Terms for Midwest Farmers." AS, 33 (1958), 260-65. Reprinted in A Linguistics Reader. Ed. Graham Wilson. New York: Harper and Row, 1967. p. 228-35.

This article notes that bushwhacker is still in use in southern Manitoba and in Ontario as a pejorative term for a farmer. There was one occurrence, in Sprague, Man., of habitant, with a "near-French" pronunciation, in the same sense.

Allen, Harold B. Cont'd.

014. __________. "Some Problems in Editing the Linguistic Atlas of the Upper Midwest," in Dialectology: Problems and Perspectives. Ed. Lorraine H. Burghardt. Knoxville: Univ. of Tennessee, 1971. p. 54-79.

The maps at the end of this article give information about 11 lexical items in Estevan, Sask., 9 in Killarney, Man., 7 in Sprague, Man., 2 in Fort Francis, Ont., and 3 in Fort William, Ont.

015. __________. "Two Dialects in Contact." AS, 48 (1973), 54-66.

Although mainly devoted to dialects of AE, in its maps and text this article gives information about 5 lexical items in CE.

016. __________, and Gary N. Underwood, eds. Readings in American Dialectology. New York: Appleton, Century, Crofts, 1971.

This anthology contains items 126 and 326 of this Bibliography.

017. Allen, H. D. "Canadian English." Gazette (Montreal), 15 Apr. 1967, p. 23.

This review of SD mentions the number of its entries and outlines their content. It notes SD's claim to be "Canadian" and cites 8 entries in support of this. It gives 3 examples of SD's orthographical catholicity and 2 of its phonological liberality. SD's inclusion of regional forms is also noted.

018. Allen, Robert Thomas. "If we keep on doing our thing and blowing our mind we'll--uh--forget how to talk." [In table of contents as "Say It Like It Is--in English."] Maclean's Magazine, Sept. 1969, p. 68.

In this article, the author discusses 32 slang words and catch phrases he has observed in use in Canada. He disapproves of them as confusing, imprecise, and distracting.

019. Anderson, Doris. "On getting unhooked from hip." Chatelaine, Apr. 1971, p. 1.

This article lists 57 initialisms, acronyms, slang words, and catch phrases which, it implies, are in use in Canada. The older meanings of 30 of the examples are given.

020. Anon. "Avis Chief Editor of Dictionary." Kingston Whig-Standard, 7 Dec. 1967, p. 45.

This review of DCHP gives a brief history of its making and notes the varied origins of the words it contains.

021. ________. "Canada Won't Even Import American Spelling." Evening Sun (Baltimore), 2nd ed. 5 Aug. 1931, p. 19.

This item notes that three Canadian learned societies have opted for English spelling and cites 4 words whose BE spelling is different from their AE spelling.

022. ________. "Canada's English can be confusing to outsiders." Telegram (Toronto), 27 Mar. 1967, p. 29.

This reports on a paper read to the Ontario Educational Association by P. D. Drysdale on behalf of Walter S. Avis. It lists 17 semantic and 4 phonological Canadianisms and notes Avis's plea that CE be taught in schools and universities.

023. ________. "C.B.C. Uses Two Dictionaries: Can't Go Wrong, Critic Told." Toronto Daily Star, 13 Jan. 1949, p. 29.

This records one critic's objections to 5 items, phonological and syntactical, stated to be common in the speech of CBC announcers; it then gives the CBC's reply, exemplified in 2 other pronunciations. The CBC claims it follows "an Oxford and a Webster's dictionary," and also monitors its announcers' pronunciation and delivery.

024. ________. "Canadian Dictionary Gets Cool Reception." Chronicle-Herald (Halifax, N.S.), 24 Apr. 1959, p. 28.

The "cool reception" was accorded to a proposal from the Ontario Department of Education. Opponents of the idea of a Canadian dictionary found the combination of an American and

Anon. Cont'd.

a British dictionary adequate. For some words, e.g., hockey, a dictionary was held to be unnecessary.

025. __________. "Canadian Dictionary Planned." Edmonton Journal, 13 June 1958, p. 33.

This report of a paper by M.H. Scargill gives the editorial board, the procedures, and the principles behind the DCE project then in preparation. The report cites 16 Canadianisms and draws attention to their varied linguistic origins.

026. __________. "Canadian English Language Project Report." Canadian Council of Teachers of English Newsletter, 4:1 (Winter 1971), 2.

This is a brief progress report on the SCE.

027. __________. "Canadian English Subject of Address at University." Kingston Whig-Standard, 20 Nov. 1958, p. 37.

This report of a talk by Walter S. Avis admits that both AE and BE have strongly influenced CE, but claims that CE is still unique. It cites 60 lexical and 15 phonological items peculiar to CE to prove this. Canadian acceptance of both BE and AE spelling is mentioned, and the function of the then envisaged DCE is outlined.

028. __________. "Canadian English taught at or in Fredericton." Star Weekly (Montreal), 19 Feb. 1972, p. 7.

This article mentions 4 lexical items noted in the Maritimes and thought to be contrastive with synonyms in the rest of Canada.

029. __________. "A Canadian Language?" Edmonton Journal, 8 Apr. 1957, p. 4.

This report of an interview with Walter S. Avis lists 15 words or phrases which Avis regarded as Canadianisms whose existence showed the need for a Canadian dictionary. The writer of the article denies this need on the grounds that most of the words cited are current only in Canada or are

Anon. Cont'd.

borrowings from Amerindian or Eskimo or refer to uniquely Canadian institutions.

030. ________. "The Canadian Language." Nelson Daily News (Nelson, B.C.), 8 Sept. 1959, p. 4.

This comment on DCE, then in preparation, questions whether there is enough CE for it to be recognizable. It regards most Canadianisms as localisms or colloquialisms, illustrating the latter. It also objects to the claim that British Columbia English is influenced by AE.

031. ________. "The Canadian Language." Time, Canada Ed., 21 July 1958, p. 10.

This article tells how M.H. Scargill first joined the DCE project. It gives 20 examples of lexical Canadianisms and also mentions spelling and pronunciation.

032. ________. "The Canadian Languages." CBC Times, 3-9 Mar. 1957, p. 3.

This report of an interview with Walter S. Avis instances 1 phonological and 12 lexical Canadianisms ignored by contemporary dictionaries. These demonstrate the need for a Canadian dictionary.

033. ________. "Canadian Speech Bumpy, Flat, Dramatics Professor Claims." Globe and Mail (Toronto), 18 Apr. 1952, p. 17.

This article describes a paper given by George E. Buckley. The speaker lamented the absence of a standard speech in Canada. He charged that the CE /r/ distorted Canadian speech, instancing the various pronunciations of Toronto.

034. ________. "Canadian Trainees Coining Language All Their Own." Toronto Daily Star, 13 Sept. 1941, p. 9.

This item reports 14 words and 9 idioms then current among Canadian servicemen in Canada.

Anon. Cont'd.

035. __________. "Canadianism Meaning." Sun-Times (Owen Sound, Ont.), 15 Dec. 1967, p. 4.

This is a reprint of "From Abatteau to Zombie" by John W. Grace, q.v.

036. __________. "Canadianisms Catalogued." Times-Journal (St. Thomas, Ont.), 12 Dec. 1967, p. 4.

This is a reprint of "From Abatteau to Zombie" by John W. Grace, q.v.

037. __________. "Canadianisms Defined in Unique Dictionary." Feliciter (Canadian Library Association, Ottawa), Apr. 1968, p. 26-27.

This article gives a very brief outline of DCHP's history, exemplifies some entries, and notes its wide human appeal.

038. __________. "Canajan, Eh?" Weekend Magazine, 2 Feb. 1974, p. 18-20.

This is an excerpting of 39 items from Canajan, Eh? by Mark M. Orkin, q.v.

039. __________. "Cariboo Slum Holds Its Place in British Columbia." Quesnel News (Quesnel, B.C.), 13 Dec. 1967, p. 2.

After a brief biography of Charles Crate, an editor of DCHP, this article gives Crate's outline of the procedures of etymological research. It cites the Amerindian etymology of several British Columbia expressions and quotes 8 others of English origin. DCHP is given brief, favorable mention as a "dictionary of dialect."

040. __________. "Climbing fool's hill." Valley Visitor (Woodstock, N.B.: Bugle Press), 2:1 (8-21 July [1974?]), 11. Reprinted in Nos. 2, 3, 4, and 5 of vol. 2.

This article claims the phrase climbing fool's hill 'committing the follies of youth' as peculiar to New Brunswick.

Anon. Cont'd.

041. ________. "A Comedy in a Flat." Canadian Magazine, 64 (Feb.-Dec. 1925), 95-96.

Though mainly devoted to discussing dictionaries' rules, this article remarks on the rarity of the "broad or Italian 'a'" among speakers on the West Coast.

042. ________. "Commons asks true definition of Francophone." Globe and Mail (Toronto), 20 Mar. 1971, p. 10.

This article reports 3 different definitions used in the Canadian House of Commons for the term francophone.

043. ________. Description of Speaking Canadian English by Mark M. Orkin. NADS, 4:3 (Nov. 1972), 12.

This description of Mark M. Orkin's book consists mainly of a list of the material in each chapter of the original, as recorded in the table of contents therein.

044. ________. "Dialect Colors Newfoundland Speech: A 'Hagorid' to Dictionary Compilers." Evening Telegram (St. John's, Nfld.), 26 Nov. 1957, p. 8.

This report of a talk by G.M. Story considers "popular" as opposed to "educated" Newfoundland dialect. The sound laws of the popular dialect are regular, as 5 examples show. Its grammar is at once preservative and innovative, as 8 examples show. So, too, is its vocabulary, as 23 examples show. Finally, 9 examples show the "vigour and expressiveness" of its idioms.

045. ________. "Dialects Dictionary Project Begins Here." Evening Telegram (St. John's, Nfld.), 19 June 1956, p. 3.

This account of a paper by G.M. Story on the then projected Newfoundland dialect dictionary shows its importance by giving 10 examples of words peculiar to Newfoundland. The methods of data collection are described and 9 examples are used to illustrate the difficulties in presenting the material. The dictionary's intent of defining the currency of each word is also mentioned.

Anon. Cont'd.

046. __________. "Dictionary To Be Truly Canadian." Kingston Whig-Standard, 2 Oct. 1964, p. 15.

This description of the then forthcoming DCHP names its editors and notes its principles of word-selection and its historical intent. It cites 4 Canadianisms it will include.

047. __________. "Editorial Idearama." Kingston Whig-Standard, 3 May 1956, p. 4.

After commenting on the past vogue for coinages in -ium and -eria, this article gives 3 examples of coinages with -rama and suggests 7 more calculated to end the fad.

048. __________. "English as She Is Spuk." Canadian Magazine, 63 (May-Oct. 1924), 256.

This article notes 1 difference of idiom, 1 of spelling, 7 of word, and 5 of phrase, between CE and BE.

049. __________. "Fliers Use English Terms: Soldiers Say 'Baloney.'" Toronto Daily Star, 7 June 1943, p. 13.

Citing 4 Briticisms from "recently published letters from R.C.A.F. men," this article speculates on the possibility that Canadians serving overseas may adopt English terms. A letter from a Canadian soldier refuting this idea is also excerpted.

050. __________. "Folklore Animals," DN, 5 (1918-1927), 188.

This article lists the names of 13 imaginary animals and gives the districts in which 5 of the names are said to be in use.

051. __________. "Haultain--the Observer." Canadian Magazine, 22 (Nov. 1903-Apr. 1904), 205.

This article lists 6 slang expressions current in CE around the turn of the century.

Anon. Cont'd.

052. __________. "Ignite Me or I'll Belt You With My African Soupbone." Toronto Daily Star, 25 Jan. 1950, p. 25.

This article reports 30 words and phrases in use among Canada's "hoodlum gangs."

053. __________. "The Interim Word." Time, Canada Ed., 23 Mar. 1962, p. 12.

This review gives some statistics on DCCD and a brief account of its authorship. It reports on and exemplifies its doctrines of spelling, usage, and pronunciation. It also notes DCCD's inclusion of Canadianisms in both English and French and cites 12 examples of these.

054. __________. "Liveyers' Language." Time, Canada Ed., 5 Nov. 1956, p. 18.

Including that in the title, this article cites 18 Newfoundland words and 3 Newfoundland phrases. It describes the diversity of etymology and the antiquity of many Newfoundlandisms. It derives their existence from the outports' remoteness and notes that this is ceasing but notes also G.M. Story's plans to preserve such words in a Newfoundland dictionary.

055. __________. "A local expression." Capital Visitor (Woodstock, N.B.: Bugle Press), 1:4 (7-20 Aug. [1971?]), 7.

This article records the use of some and right as adverbs in New Brunswick.

056. __________. "Local figures of speech." Elm City Visitor (Woodstock, N.B.: Bugle Press), 1:1 (30 June-13 July 1973), 3. Reprinted in next 4 nos. of vol. 1. Reprinted in Valley Visitor (Woodstock, N.B.: Bugle Press), 3:1 (29 June 1974), 16, and in several nos. of vol. 4 of this paper.

This article records 2 pronunciations, 1 word, and 2 phrases common in the speech of New Brunswick.

Anon. Cont'd.

057. __________. "Mr. Hoover at the Microphone." Ottawa Journal, 13 Aug. 1932, p. 6.

Characterizing Mr. Hoover's speech as unimpressive and as "Americanese," this article fears lest radio may spread this into Canada.

058. __________. "A New Language: Canadian English." New York Times, 29 Nov. 1959, p. 148.

This article announces the CLA's plans to replace British and American dictionaries with a rehandling of the Thorndike-Barnhart dictionary. It then glances at the origins of Canadianisms. After giving 7 phonological, 7 lexical, and 9 orthographical examples showing CE standing between BE and AE, the article ends with 1 phonological and 16 lexical "true" Canadianisms.

059. __________. "Non-Broncho English." Time, Canada Ed., 20 Sept. 1963, p. 12.

After "translating" a fictional paragraph containing 9 Canadianisms, this article records the inclusion in Funk and Wagnalls Dictionary of 600 Canadianisms from Walter S. Avis's collection and exemplifies the sources whence he obtained them. It also records the start of work for the DCHP.

060. __________. "Of Canadian Flavor." Daily Colonist (Victoria, B.C.), 7 June 1966, p. 4.

This article refers to M.H. Scargill's comment on the large number of Canadianisms in CE. It adds that the absence of most of these from standard dictionaries has created the need for the DCHP, then in preparation, and it summarizes the editorial principles of DCHP.

061. __________. "Of Hootch, Hydro and Sweets." Time, Canada Ed., 17 Nov. 1967, p. 17-18.

After commenting on Canadian linguistic inventiveness in terminology associated with liquor, this review of DCHP cites, giving their origins, 42 examples of Canadian inventiveness in wider fields. It gives a brief account of DCHP's history.

Anon. Cont'd.

062. __________. "Our Gift to English." C-I-L Oval, 37:1 (Spring 1968), 14.

This article records the history and character of DCHP and gives and exemplifies DCHP's definition of a Canadianism. It then notes and exemplifies P.D. Drysdale's view that Canadians are linguistically inventive.

063. __________. "Out of Favor." Time, Canada Ed., 9 June 1975, p. 7.

This notes the preference in CE for spellings in -or over spellings in -our.

064. __________. "Parliament Goes Hollywood." Ottawa Journal, 7 Apr. 1934, p. 6.

This notes the disappearance from Parliament of "Gladstonian . . . ponderosity of language " and the appearance in its stead of Americanisms, of which the article gives 3 examples from general usage and 3 more from the cinema.

065. __________. "Pronunciation." Ottawa Evening Journal, 8 Dec. 1939, p. 6.

This repeats some paragraphs from "On Pronunciation in Particular and Sticking One's Chin Out in General" by G.H.C., q.v.

066. __________. "Related Studies to Speed Compiling New Dictionary." Edmonton Journal, 30 July 1958, p. 3.

This report of a talk by M.H. Scargill outlines the plans for the DCE, then in progress. It states the objective of the production of DCHP: to emphasize that CE is distinct from BE. It mentions some of the difficulties, giving 2 examples of words with 2 spellings, and it outlines the principles of word-selection for the DCE.

067. __________. "Report on the Canadian English Project." EngQ, 3:3 (Fall 1970), 56.

This report names some of the planning committee for the SCE and outlines the character of the project.

Anon. Cont'd.

068. __________. Review of A Dictionary of Canadianisms on Historical Principles, Walter S. Avis, Ed.-in-Chief. TLS, 26 Feb. 1970, p. 233.

The review debates whether there is such a thing as CE and then praises DCHP's clarification of the Canadian contribution to the English lexicon. It contrasts DCHP's concept of Canadianism favorably with Mitford M. Mathews's concept of Americanism. Finally, it regrets that DCHP's editors relied only on written records.

069. __________. "Say It in Canadian." Toronto Daily Star, 9 Feb. 1957, p. 6.

This article records the CLA's intention of producing a distinctively Canadian dictionary, notes the inadequacy for Canadians of British and American dictionaries, and gives 16 lexical examples and 1 phonological example of Canadianisms.

070. __________. "Says Canada Needs Own Dictionary." Edmonton Journal, 4 Aug. 1961, p. 30.

This report of a talk by Walter S. Avis points out that CE needs its own dictionary, both for spellings and for definitions. It gives 4 instances wherein CE differs from AE and 4 wherein CE differs from BE.

071. __________. "Several definitions you should know." Brunswickan (Univ. of New Brunswick student newspaper), 7 Sept. 1973, p. 9.

This article gives 60 examples of slang words and phrases current among, although not necessarily limited to, students at the University of New Brunswick.

072. __________. "Ship Talk." Maclean's Magazine, 15 Mar. 1942, front cover.

This glossary lists and defines 96 Royal Canadian Navy slang words and expressions.

073. __________. "Slang and Twang." Moose Jaw News, 1 Feb. 1884, p. 2.

After claiming that most Canadians can be located by their

Anon. Cont'd.

speech, this article deprecates the possible introduction into the Canadian Northwest of alleged American nasality and slanginess and gives 7 examples of the latter.

074. ________. "Speaking as a Canadian." Canada Council Bulletin, No. 13 (Autumn 1962), p. 1-5.

After pointing out how difficult it is to answer the question "Is there a distinctly Canadian way of speaking?" this article outlines the work then done on CE. Special mention is made of lexicography in Newfoundland and of linguistic geography there and elsewhere, particularly in the Maritimes. The progress of DCHP and the publication of DCCD are noted, and the functions of the University of Montreal's Lexicographic Research Centre are discussed.

075. ________. "These Definitions Will Become Everyday Words." Brunswickan (Univ. of New Brunswick student newspaper), 6 Sept. 1974, p. 5.

This is a reprint, with 3 fewer examples, of "Several definitions you should know" Anon., q.v.

076. ________. "Time to Recognize Mukluks and Herring Chokers." London Free Press, 6 Feb. 1957, p. 6.

This report of a paper by Walter S. Avis points out that Canadians have their own dialect of English and cites 4 lexical items and 1 phonological item to support this. The fact that contemporary dictionaries ignore these and other Canadianisms creates the need for a Canadian dictionary.

077. ________. "Two Dictionaries Needed By The Canadians." Evening Sun (Baltimore), 5 Oct. 1937, p. 21.

This article draws attention to the CE use of coal oil in place of the BE paraffin and the AE kerosene.

078. ________. "Wanted: Canadian Words." Sunday Telegram (Toronto), 7 Apr. 1957, p. 13B.

This article reports Walter S. Avis's definition of Canadianisms and gives examples of 18 of them.

Anon. Cont'd.

079. _________. "Watch Your Language." Shell News (Montreal), July-Aug. 1957, p. 8-11.

Basing the need for a bilingual dictionary on Canada's possession of two distinct languages, this progress report on DCCD follows its citation of 17 Canadianisms by a description of the University of Montreal's Language Research Centre. It notes and exemplifies geographical movement and regional semantic variation of words and illustrates how the needs for new words arise. It mentions that DCCD will be prescriptive as well as descriptive and closes by citing some reactions to the proposed dictionary.

080. _________. "Watson Redux." Time, Canada Ed., 24 Apr. 1972, p. 11.

This article exemplifies the American view that Canadians say "oot" for out and "aboot" for about.

081. _________. "We Speak Canadian." Weekend Magazine, 25 Nov. 1967, p. 34.

This article on DCHP gives a fictional paragraph of Canadianisms, together with a brief history of DCHP, from which it excerpts 28 items.

082. _________. "We think, like, it's a poor way to, y'know, speak the language." CAB, 49:4 (Summer 1974), 18.

This article comments disapprovingly on the frequency of there, right? you know, like, and eh? as interjections in spoken CE. It also comments on the distinctive Canadian pronunciation of the diphthong exemplified in house, out, and about.

083. _________. "Well, They've Managed To Fill Three Volumes With It, So There Must Be a Canadian Way to Speak English." Canada Month, Dec. 1961, p. 13-14.

This article mentions the medial position of CE, between BE and AE, and characterizes the then forthcoming BD as the first volume of DCE. After glancing at the origins of Canadianisms and exemplifying 14 of them, the article describes the history and methodology of DCE.

Anon. Cont'd.

084. __________. "Word Hunters Avoid Books to Compile New Dictionary." Calgary Herald, 14 Sept. 1963, p. 20.

This article outlines the history of DCHP, then in preparation. It points out that the sources of DCHP are Canadian writings of linguistic rather than of literary value and instances two of them. The article also points out that the intention of the editors of DCHP is to record, not to arbitrate.

085. __________. "The World of Nursing." Canadian Nurse, 60 (1964), 475-77.

This is a glossary of 31 Newfoundland words, all recorded in Historic Newfoundland by L.E.F. English, q.v., as is noted in "Bibliography of Writings on Newfoundland English" by William J. Kirwin, q.v.

086. Anon. (CP). "Bilingual Canadian Dictionary Aimed At Compiling Special Words and Meanings." Kingston Whig-Standard, 27 Nov. 1958, p. 11.

After a comment on the failure of dictionaries to explain CE terms, this article describes the background work from which DCCD, then in preparation, emerged. The qualifications of the editors, their methods, and their concern with Eskimo and Amerindian words (exemplified) are all mentioned.

087. __________. "Canadian-isms Recorded." Winnipeg Tribune, 31 July 1959, p. 3.

This article reports an interview with Walter S. Avis, echoing the latter's view that "British and American dictionaries do not reflect Canadian usage satisfactorily," noting his observation of some 10 Canadianisms, and reporting his explanation from Canada's history of the quality of CE.

088. __________. "Canadians Have Own Language." Kingston Whig-Standard, 23 Nov. 1967, p. 50.

This article records M.H. Scargill's comment that CE differs from BE and from AE and cites 17 examples he gives to support his view.

Anon. (CP). Cont'd.

089. __________. "From splane [sic] to mukluks." Province (Vancouver), 16 June 1958, p. 4.

This report of a paper by M.H. Scargill describes the research planned to support the DCE, characterizes two of the dictionaries proposed, and notes that 25,000 words are already on file. It cites 17 specimen Canadianisms and defines 10 of them.

090. __________. "Hunt On for Words For New Dictionary." Ottawa Journal, 20 Mar. 1957, p. 11.

This report of an interview with Walter S. Avis records his view that CE is part of the national identity and quotes 19 words or phrases peculiar to Canada and 3 with meanings peculiar to Canada. Regionalisms, of which 4 are quoted, show the need for a Canadian dictionary. The CLA's support for the project is mentioned.

091. __________. "In the Book Corner." Guide (Port Hope, Ont.), 29 Jan. 1968, p. 2 and 6.

This review of DCHP exemplifies its etymologizing and its precision in defining. It notes that DCHP's contents are not exclusively pure Canadianisms and outlines DCHP's history.

092. __________. "Linguists Receive Report on Canadian Dictionary." Kingston Whig-Standard, 14 June 1958, p. 19.

This is a slightly abbreviated version of "From splane to mukluks" Anon. (CP), q.v.

093. __________. "Many Theories Advanced Concerning Origin of Name Canada." Evening News (New Glasgow, N.S.), 25 Jan. 1968, p. 9.

This is a reprint of "In the Book Corner" Anon. (CP), q.v.

094. __________. "May Have Dictionary of Our Own." Kingston-Whig-Standard, 5 Feb. 1957, p. 1.

This account of a talk by Walter S. Avis records the start

Anon. (CP). Cont'd.

of the DCE project, gives 1 lexical example of regional variation, and cites 5 Canadianisms.

095. __________. "Not What You Say, How You Say It: Joe Buggins Will Grab the Dooey." Toronto Daily Star, 9 June 1945, p. 8.

Claiming that philologists have observed that CE naval slang varies from ship to ship, this article gives 20 examples of slang; but all are apparently from one ship.

096. __________. "Professor Sets Himself a Task." Edmonton Journal, 20 Mar. 1957, p. 10.

This is the same item as "Hunt On for Words For New Dictionary" Anon. (CP), q.v.

097. __________. "Ulster Dialect Lingers Long, Educator Finds." Montreal Star, 12 June 1959, p. 14.

This is a report of a paper by R.J. Gregg. It cites 7 Ulster dialect words still current in spoken if not in written CE.

098. __________. "Victorian Prudishness Eliminated In New Edition Of Oxford English Dictionary." Daily Gleaner (Fredericton), 1 Nov. 1972, p. 20.

This review of the Supplement A-G to OED notes that butt-end, Canadien, and Galbraithian are recorded as Canadianisms therein.

099. __________. "Will Fliers['] Little Sprogs Always Talk Rhubarb?" Toronto Daily Star, 11 Apr. 1944, p.4.

This article records 29 slang words and phrases used by the Royal Canadian Air Force.

100. Anon. (R.C.A.F. News Service). "'Shove Ha'penny' and P.M. Tea On Way Here via Johnny Canuck." Toronto Daily Star, 24 Mar. 1943, p. 9.

This article gives 11 examples of slang and standard BE said to be common in the CE of the Royal Canadian Air Force.

101. Arbour, Marcy. "New Assortment of Canadianisms." Windsor Star, 18 May 1968, p. 10D.

This review of DCHP quotes that dictionary's definition of a Canadianism; it laments that DCHP is "not nearly long enough." It notes DCHP's topographical, political, and historical content, as also its content of Indian folklore.

102. Avis, Walter S. "A Bibliography of Writings on Canadian English." JCLA, 1, No. 2, Regular Series (Oct. 1955), 19-20.

This lists 35 articles on CE.

103. ________. A Bibliography of Writings on Canadian English (1857-1965). Toronto: W. J. Gage, 1965.

This work lists 103 articles and reprints in scholarly journals, 44 in newspapers and other non-scholarly publications, 15 books, 2 pamphlets, and 4 theses dealing wholly or partly with CE. (Each of these items was considered in preparing this present Bibliography.)

104. ________. "Canadian English," in Funk and Wagnalls Standard College Dictionary. New York: Funk and Wagnalls, 1963. p. xv-xvi. Reprinted in Funk and Wagnalls Standard College Dictionary: Canadian Edition. Toronto: Longmans Canada, 1963. p. xvii. Reprinted in Funk and Wagnalls Standard Dictionary of the English Language: International Edition, combined with Britannica World Language Dictionary. Chicago: Encyclopædia Britannica, 1966. p. xiii-xiv. Reprinted in Funk and Wagnalls Standard Encyclopedic Dictionary. Chicago: J.G. Ferguson, 1965. p. 915. Reprinted in Funk and Wagnalls Standard College Dictionary: Canadian Edition. Toronto: Fitzhenry and Whiteside, 1973. p. xv-xvi.

This is mainly a reprint of "Canadian English and Native Dictionaries" by Walter S. Avis, q.v. This version lacks the first and the last two paragraphs of the original, and the selection of examples is updated. The selection of examples is again updated for the 1973 reprint.

Avis, Walter S. Cont'd.

105. __________. "Canadian English," in The Senior Dictionary. Ed. Walter S. Avis and others (q.v.). p. vi-ix. Reprinted in The Gage Canadian Dictionary. Ed. Walter S. Avis and others (q.v.). p. vi-ix. Reprinted, in part, in Profile of a Nation by A. Dawe. Toronto: Macmillan, 1969. p. 34-35.

The author first notes that CE differs from AE, citing as evidence 5 lexical and 7 phonological items; he distinguishes it likewise from BE, citing 7 lexical and 7 phonological items. CE is the product of Canada's settlement history: originally American, and with continuing American influence and a common ecology, but with strong British immigration as well. Besides this, there are many native Canadianisms; the author cites 68 lexical items originating in Canada, 18 with special meanings in CE and 19 words whose Canadian pronunciation is generally ignored in imported dictionaries. In spelling, CE shows a blend of BE (9 examples) and AE (7 examples), although the latter is becoming more popular.

106. __________. "Canadian English and Native Dictionaries," in Education: A Collection of Essays on Canadian Education. Vol. 3, 1958-1960. Toronto: W.J. Gage, 1960. p. 15-19.

Starting with two anecdotes distinguishing CE from AE and BE, the author outlines the socio-historical origins of the Canadian amalgam. He cites 99 Canadianisms, including regional names, loanwords, regionalisms, animal and plant names, and words from politics and sport. Canadian pronunciation is shown by a further 19 examples. The criterion of correctness should be the usage of educated native Canadians. The Canadian duality in spelling is also mentioned and exemplified. The two final paragraphs outline the CLA's dictionary project and ask help therewith.

107. __________. "III. Canadian English/Anglo-Canadien." JCLA, 2:2 (1956), 82.

This is a bibliography listing 2 books and 10 articles bearing on CE.

108. __________. "III. Canadian English/Anglo-Canadien." JCLA, 3 (1957), 97.

This is a bibliography listing 1 book and 17 articles bearing on CE.

Avis, Walter S. Cont'd

109. ________. "III. Canadian English/Anglo-Canadien." JCLA, 4 (1958), 107-08.

This is a bibliography listing 16 articles and 2 theses bearing on CE.

110. ________. "III. Canadian English/Anglo-Canadien." JCLA, 6 (1960), 87-88.

This is a bibliography listing 15 articles bearing on CE.

111. ________. "III. Canadian English [bibliography]." CJL, 7 (1962), 115-16.

This is a bibliography listing 6 articles bearing on CE.

112. ________. "III. Canadian English [bibliography]." CJL, 9 (1964), 120-23.

This is a bibliography listing 8 books, 3 pamphlets, 1 thesis, and 50 articles bearing on CE.

113. ________. "II. Canadian English [bibliography]." CJL, 15 (1969), 70-73.

See item 619.

114. ________. "Canadian English: Language and Linguistics," in On Canadian Literature 1806-1960. Comp. Reginald Eyre Watters and Inglis Freeman Bell. Toronto: Univ. of Toronto, 1966. p. 13-19

This bibliography repeats 136 items from A Bibliography of Writings on Canadian English (1857-1965) by Walter S. Avis, q.v., and adds 13 more items, of which 9 are on onomastics.

115. ________. "Canadian English Merits a Dictionary." Culture, 18 (1957), 245-56.

This article outlines the socio-historical background of

Avis, Walter S. Cont'd.

CE, "a dialect which resembles American English in some respects and British in others, and which includes a good deal that is singularly Canadian." To show this, the author gives over 100 examples and suggests that these and similar words should make up a Canadian dictionary, as they are either ignored or poorly handled in contemporary dictionaries. Moreover, a country-wide survey should be made to determine Canadian practice in pronunciation and spelling.

116. ________. "Canadian Lexicon in the Making." CBC Times, 24-30 Mar. 1957, p. 2.

The author claims that a good dictionary reflects the usage of the educated people in a given speech community and points out that, although CE is distinctive and important to national identity, Canadians have no choice but to seek their standard from British or American dictionaries. The shortcomings of these are exemplified by 26 lexical and 19 phonological items.

117. ________. "Canadian Spoken Here," in Looking at Language. Ed. M.H. Scargill and P.G. Penner (q.v.). p. 17-39.

After noting that CE differs in many details from BE (7 phonological and 5 lexical examples are given) and from AE (5 lexical and 5 phonological examples), the author concludes that CE is a blend of the two. An extended summary of Canada's settlement history explains why. But CE is still distinctive, as is exemplified by 24 native, 12 regional, and 16 miscellaneous lexical items. Its regional variation is shown by the 28 names for the Canada jay and by the history and semantic richness of siwash and snye, as also by its borrowing (4 examples) and its compounding (7 examples). Finally, the author notes that some Canadianisms are now of historical interest only. A Glossary of 78 entries explains Canadianisms used in the article.

118. ________. "'Darn' in 'The Clockmaker.'" AS, 26 (1951), 302-03.

The use of both darn(ed) and (e)tarnal by Sam Slick in The Clockmaker supports the theory that darn derives from (e)tarnal damnation. Slick's adverbial use of darn antedates DAE's first quotation. Slick shows also the continued use of darn as a verb.

Avis, Walter S. Cont'd.

119. ________. "Dictionaries for Canadian English." Inside the ACD, 11(1958), 2.

The author argues that CE is distinctive and that British and American dictionaries do not serve it. He exemplifies this by 28 lexical, 13 phonological, and 20 orthographical items.

120. ________. "English in Canada," in Looking at Language. Ed. M.H. Scargill and P.G. Penner. 2nd rev. ed. (q.v.). p. 64-87.

This is a more or less verbatim reprint of "Canadian Spoken Here" by the same author, q.v., with the addition of a paragraph on Canadian coinages.

121. ________. "The English Language in Canada: A Report." Current Trends in Linguistics, 10, Pt. 1 (1973), 40-74.

After an Introduction on the state of research on CE in 1954, the present position of English as dominant in a mosaic is stated and its historical origins described. Writings on CE to 1969 are reviewed, work in progress is described, and present resources for teaching and research are summarized. GCE as spoken from Toronto to British Columbia is then described on the basis of tape recordings made by the author, who cites 5 lexical, 10 phonological, 1 syntactical, and 2 idiomatic features in which GCE coincides with BE and differs from AE, and 5 lexical, 6 phonological, 3 syntactical features, and 1 idiomatic feature in which GCE coincides with AE and differs from BE. GCE is unique in 6 phonological features: the fusion of /ɔ/ and /ɑ/ as /ɑ/; the allophones of /aɪ/, /aʊ/, and /oɪ/; the domain of /æ/; the pronunciation of khaki; and of vase; the use, more frequent than in AE, of /ju/. A phonemic inventory of GCE vowels is included. The author gives 88 lexical Canadianisms and examines 1 in detail. Of 18 orthographic examples, some show agreement with BE, some agreement with AE. There is a select bibliography of 104 works on CE to 1969 and a supplementary list of another 17 background works.

122. ________. "Eskimo Words in Canadian English," in Lexicography and Dialect Geography: Festgabe for Hans Kurath. Ed. Harald Scholler and John Reidy (ZDL, Beihefte, NF, H.9. Wiesbaden: Steiner, 1973), p. 25-36.

After a brief history of the Eskimos, the author illustrates

Avis, Walter S. Cont'd.

with 9 examples the complexities of English spellings of Eskimo sounds and shows the variety in the spellings of each of the significant Eskimo phonemes. He then excerpts from DCHP 51 Eskimo words in CE.

123. ________. "Further Lexicographical Evidence from the 'Clockmaker.'" AS, 27 (1952), 16-19.

Classifying his material as (1) words antedating DAE entries designated as Americanisms, (2) words antedating DAE entries not specifically designated as Americanisms, (3) words antedating DA entries and (4) words not entered in DAE or DA and antedating OED entries, the author gives 9, 18, 14, and 30 items respectively, from Haliburton's work.

124. ________. "The Importance of Pronunciation in a Canadian Dictionary." Journal des Traducteurs--Translators' Journal, 3 (1959), 21-24.

The author first outlines the sources from which the dictionary in North America derives its prestige. He then adds that standards of correctness are usually set by the educated and cultured speakers and observes that Canadian correctness is neither wholly British nor wholly American; it is inadequately served by pronunciations in contemporary dictionaries, as 78 examples show. He suggests the research that is needed to develop a dictionary phonologically adequate for CE.

125. ________. "Linguistics." Encyclopedia Canadiana, vol. 6 (Toronto: Grolier of Canada, 1957), 145.

This article gives a roll-call of scholars who, within the area of linguistics, are working in the field of CE, and it records the founding and early development of the CLA.

126. ________. "The 'New England Short o'; A Recessive Phoneme." Language, 37 (1961), 544-58. Reprinted in Readings in American Dialectology. Ed. Harold B. Allen and Gary N. Underwood (q.v.). p. 200-15. Reprinted in A Various Language: Perspectives on American Dialects. Ed. Juanita V. Williamson and Virginia Burke (q.v.). p. 389-405.

The maps and diagrams in this article show the absence of the phoneme /ɵ/ from the speech of western New Brunswick,

Avis, Walter S. Cont'd.

as also from the Canadian-influenced speech of 2 U.S. towns on the Maine/New Brunswick border. It also notes the survival of /ɵ/ as a relic on the Canadian side of the border in the St. Lawrence Valley.

127. ________. "A Note on the Speech of Sam Slick," in <u>The Sam Slick Anthology</u>. Sel. and intro. by Reginald Eyre Watters. Toronto: Clarke, Irwin, 1969. p. xix-xxix.

The author points out that Haliburton's background acquainted him thoroughly with the common speech of Nova Scotia and of its close relative in New England. He explains in detail, mentioning 11 features and giving 68 examples, how the authors of the anthology have treated Haliburton's representation of this dialect. There is a Glossary of 35 entries.

128. ________. "Le parler anglais au Canada de nos jours." <u>Revue de l'Université Laval</u>, 16 (1961), 314-22. Reprinted in <u>Documents: L'Alliance Canadienne (AC-CA). Travaux publiés d'abord dans La Revue de l'Université Laval en 1960-1961</u>. Quebec: <u>Editions de l'Alliance Canadienne, 1961.</u> p. 51-59.

Demonstrating that CE is a mixture of AE and BE, the author gives 29 examples wherein it differs from one or the other and notes that the peculiar character of CE derives from Canada's history. CE contains many Canadianisms, of which the author cites 64. A further 57 examples show the deficiencies of contemporary dictionaries in treating these and show that a specifically Canadian dictionary is needed. The state of this project is briefly described. There is a discussion, with 31 examples, of Canadian spelling, and the article ends with a review of research on CE.

129. ________. "The Past Participle <u>Drank</u>: Standard American English?" <u>AS</u>, 28 (1953), 106-11.

This article includes statistics, based on those of the LAUSC, showing the relative infrequency of <u>drank</u> as a past participle in eastern Canada.

130. ________. "The Phonemic Segments of an Edmonton Idiolect," in <u>Studies in Linguistics in Honor of Raven I. McDavid, Jr.</u> Ed. Lawrence M. Davis. University, Ala.: Univ. of Alabama, 1972. p. 239-50. Reprinted

Avis, Walter S. Cont'd

in "Readings on Language in Canada." Ed. Ronald H. Southerland (q.v.). p. 55-71. Reprinted in Canadian English: Origins and Structures. Ed. J.K. Chambers (q.v.). p. 118-28.

The author's informant was an Edmontonian of Ontario descent, a speaker of GCE, and one "typical of his age and level of education." Each vocalic phoneme is characterized phonetically, but only those allophones which are regionally significant are specially mentioned: the most striking feature is the absence of a low back phoneme (an absence usual in GCE). The consonants being those common in NAE, only /t/ and /r/ are described in detail. Finally, the qualities of this idiolect are compared with those of GCE, and a few idiosyncrasies of the idiolect are noted.

131. __________. "Problems in Editing a Canadian Dictionary: Phonology," in Lexicography in English. Ed. Raven I. McDavid, Jr. and Audrey Duckert (q.v.). p. 110-14.

The author explains that while CE generally resembles Inland Northern AE phonologically (2 features are cited to show this), the differences make it difficult to fit CE into the Thorndike-Barnhart system of respelling. The difficulties arose mainly from 2 phonemic and 4 subphonemic features of CE. The fact that younger Canadians are losing the contrast between merry and marry, etc., and also that between whales and Wales, called for difficult decisions.

132. __________. "Problems in the Study of Canadian English." Communications et Rapports du Premier Congrès International de Dialectologie Générale. Ed. A.J. Van Windekens. 3me Partie. Louvain: Centre International de Dialectologie Générale, 1965. p. 183-91.

Giving 28 examples, the author observes that CE "while different from both British and American English is . . . a blend of both varieties" with typically Canadian additions. Citing 98 Canadianisms, he gives the reasons for this. The start of DCHP, the publication of BD and ID, and the completion of SD, all created to record such words, are recounted, and further examples are given from phonology, lexicon, and spelling to show the unsatisfactoriness of contemporary dictionaries. The author ends with a review of research on CE.

Avis, Walter S. Cont'd.

133. __________. Report of the Regional Secretary for Canada. PADS, 23 (1955), 57-58.

This report describes the then paucity of linguistic studies in Canada, outlines the work in progress, and announces the formation of the CLA.

134. __________. Report of the Regional Secretary for Canada. NADS, 3:2 (June 1971), 4-6.

This report mentions the publication of WI, and proposes revisions to the DCE series. It also mentions the SCE and some other research projects.

135. __________. "Report on the Canadian Linguistic Association." Communications et Rapports du Premier Congrès International de Dialectologie Générale. Ed. A.J. Van Windekens. 4me Partie. Louvain: Centre International de Dialectologie Générale, 1965. p. 21-22.

This report describes the founding of the CLA and gives the early history of JCLA. The width of the support for the CLA is mentioned, and the aims of the Association are outlined.

136. __________. Review of A Dictionary of Americanisms. Ed. Mitford M. Mathews. QQ, 64 (1957-58), 147-48.

The reviewer remarks that CE contains many Americanisms. He then cites 22 words claimed as Americanisms but in fact possibly Canadianisms. He notes that the dictionary has Canadian works listed in its sources and gives 8 Canadian antedatings from these.

137. __________. Review of A Dictionary of American Slang. Comp. Harold Wentworth and Stuart Berg Flexner. CJL, 8 (1962), 47-49.

This review cites 2 words labelled as archaic or obsolete in this dictionary but still current in CE. It lists a further 23 either omitted from the dictionary or wrongly defined in it.

Avis, Walter S. Cont'd.

138. __________. Review of The Pronunciation of English in the Atlantic States by Hans Kurath and Raven I. McDavid, Jr. CJL, 11 (1965), 63-70.

The reviewer points out that the work reviewed gives evidence for a low back unrounded vowel in daughter in Ontario. He also mentions that, although Map 133 discusses the word because, the data presented are insufficient for any decision about the phoneme in the second syllable of this word in CE.

139. __________, (Part author). "[Slang in] Canada." Encyclopedia Britannica. Chicago: Benton, 1967, p. 625.

The 65 examples of Canadian slang in this article were provided by Walter S. Avis.

140. __________. "So Eh? is Canadian, Eh?" CJL, 17 (1972), 89-104.

Using a randomly selected corpus of 41 British, 26 American, and 28 Canadian authors' works, together with newspapers, magazines, and speech, the author assembles and classifies syntactically 87 examples of the use of eh?; 35 examples are British, 16 American, and 36 Canadian. He concludes that eh? is no Canadianism: "it did not originate in Canada and is not peculiar to the English spoken in Canada." However, it has a high incidence in CE, especially as a colorless space-filler.

141. __________. "Speech Differences Along the Ontario-United States Border," in Canadian English: Origins and Structures. Ed. J.K. Chambers (q.v.). p. 67-77.

This is a slightly revised version of items 142 and 143, q.v.

142. __________. "Speech Differences Along the Ontario-United States Border: I. Vocabulary." JCLA, 1, No. 1, (Oct. 1954), 13-18.

Based on responses from 165 informants and on LAUSC data, this study shows 14 lexical differences between Ontario speech and American speech, but concludes that Ontario speech is an extension of the Northern dialect of AE, though forming a distinct sub-area thereof. The main differences probably rise from Canadian generalizing of Briticisms.

Avis, Walter S. Cont'd.

143. ________. "Speech Differences Along the Ontario-United States Border: II. Grammar and Syntax." JCLA, 1, No. 1, Regular Series (Mar. 1955), 14-19.

Based on data described in item 142 above, this study shows: 1 American Northernism dominant, 2 surviving, and 1 spreading; 3 Briticisms dominant and 1 recessive; and 2 American Midlandisms dominant. The article also demonstrates the close relationship between the contrasting settlement patterns in eastern and western Ontario and the correspondingly contrasting speech patterns.

144. ________. "Speech Differences Along the Ontario-United States Border: III. Pronunciation." JCLA, 2:2 (Oct. 1956), 41-59.

Based on LAUSC data and a rime-word questionnaire, this study shows that no informant consistently followed either BE or AE usage. The author discusses 31 features of speech, illustrated by 86 examples. Usage is commonly divided, but 4 features (4 examples) are shown to be typically Canadian; 12 features (14 examples) follow British, and 7 features (23 examples) favour American practice. The presence of /r/ in the CE pronunciation of khaki is discussed, and the need for more research on some features of Canadian pronunciation is indicated.

145. ________. "The Speech of Sam Slick." M.A. thesis. Queen's Univ., Kingston, Ont., 1950.

This thesis first justifies the claim that the speech of Nova Scotia differed little from the "Yankee" dialect of Sam Slick. A chapter on phonology discusses the 17 stressed vocalics, including Haliburton's spellings of each, and comments on the unstressed vowels and the consonants. Under grammar and syntax are discussed the parts of speech and the double negative, etc. The chapter on vocabulary measures the evidence from Haliburton's work against contemporary lexical data.

146. ________. "Why a Canadian Dictionary?" Speaking of Dictionaries, No. 1. Toronto: Gage Educational Publishing [1966]. p. 1-4.

Basically an expansion and updating of "Canadian English and Native Dictionaries" by Walter S. Avis, q.v., this article adds that to claim CE as a language separate from that spoken by Britons, Americans, and others is a nationalistic distortion of the word language.

Avis, Walter S. Cont'd.

147. __________. "Word Ending!" Letter to the editor. Kingston Whig-Standard, 10 May 1956, p. 4.

After pointing out that the suffix -rama means 'a view of' and citing 3 examples to prove this, the writer gives the origin of the suffix and uses 4 examples to trace its history to 1940. Since then, the success of cinerama has led to the present widespread use of the suffix, shown by 23 examples.

148. __________, Ed.-in-Chief. A Concise Dictionary of Canadianisms. Toronto: Gage Educational Publishing, 1973.

Produced by the same Editorial Board, this work is an abridgment of DCHP, made by excluding the bibliography and by omitting many obsolete and specialized words. The front matter is varied only by the updating of the selection of examples in the introduction. There are about 5,000 entries.

149. __________, __________. A Dictionary of Canadianisms on Historical Principles. Toronto: W.J. Gage, 1967.

This fourth volume of DCE was produced with the aid of an Editorial Board consisting of Charles Crate, P.D. Drysdale, Douglas Leechman, M.H. Scargill, and, until 1960, C.J. Lovell. The preface outlines the development of the dictionary. The introduction gives the purpose of the dictionary and explains the word Historical as meaning that every entry is supported by dated evidence from written sources. It defines a Canadianism as a word, expression, or meaning native to Canada or distinctive of Canadian usage. It also comments on the Canadian vocabulary. The dictionary has about 10,000 entries, supported as described. There is an extensive bibliography.

150. __________, P.D. Drysdale, R.J. Gregg, and M.H. Scargill, eds. The Gage Canadian Dictionary. Toronto: Gage Educational Publishing, 1973.

This is SD in either paperback or hard-cover format with a considerable number of Canadianisms added.

151. __________, __________, __________, and __________, eds. The Senior Dictionary. Toronto: Gage Educational Publishing, 1967. Rev. and updated, 1973.

This third volume of DCE is designed for use in high school and beyond. The front matter includes an introduction,

Avis, Walter S. and others. Cont'd.

describing the dictionary's background and method, and an essay "Canadian English" by Walter S. Avis, q.v. It has also a guide to the dictionary, which describes how to locate an entry and details the parts of an entry, including its etymologies and synonym lists. The entries, about 90,000 in number, reflect Canadian usage and hence give alternative spellings and pronunciations and include many Canadianisms. Many definitions are exemplified by sentences, and some entries are provided with illustrations.

152. __________, R.J. Gregg, C.J. Lovell, and M.H. Scargill, eds. *The Beginning Dictionary*. Toronto: W.J. Gage, 1962.

This first volume of DCE is designed for grades 4 and 5. The front matter includes a simple pronunciation system, notes to the teacher, and 67 lessons on how to use your dictionary. The entries, about 20,000 in number, reflect Canadian usage, as in *SD*. The definitions are simple and are clearly exemplified in sentences. Some are accompanied by line drawings.

153. __________, __________, and M.H. Scargill, eds. *The Intermediate Dictionary*. Toronto: W.J. Gage, 1963.

This second volume of DCE is designed for grades 6 to 9. The front matter includes a simple pronunciation system, sections on how to use this dictionary, how to find a word, how to find a meaning, how to use the pronunciations, how to use the dictionary for spelling, and on common spellings of English. The entries, about 64,000 in number, reflect Canadian usage, as in *SD*. Many definitions are exemplified in sentences, and some entries are provided with illustrations.

154. Ayearst, Morley. "A Note on Canadian Speech." *AS*, 14 (1939), 231-33.

In this article, the author, after asking whether CE is distinct from AE, states that some Canadian stress habits, the Canadian allophones of /aʊ/, the dominance of /ju/, and the retention, with some exceptions, of BE spellings, all help to set CE apart from AE. In some lexical and syntactic features, CE is said to approximate AE. After suggesting explanations for the Canadian duality, the author concludes that CE must be regarded as a variant of AE.

155. Ayre, Robert. "Remember Augustus." *SatN*, 25 May 1940, p. 24.

The author attacks slang contractions, exemplifying 4, and assails the dropping of *and* from compound numbers. So, too, he objects to the omission of *the*, though this is not exemplified.

156. Ayres, H.M., and H.C. Greet. "American Speech Records." *AS*, 5 (1930), 333-57.

In 1927-28, the authors made a Victor Talking Machine record of "Grip the Rat " from a Kitchener, Ont., informant whose biography is given and whose speech traits are exemplified. In 1929, 2 Speak-O-Phone recordings were made, 1 from Toronto and 1 from "Ontario."

157. Bähr, Dieter. "Die englische Sprache in Kanada," in *Standard English und seine geographische Varianten*. *Munich: Wilhelm Fink, 1974.* p. 238-63.

Through 11 CE spellings, the author shows the influence of AE and BE on CE. He cites 12 phonological features (34 examples) and the pronunciation of 14 words to show the dominance of AE. In grammar, 3 examples show the like. In vocabulary, 22 examples show the dual influence, 10 show Canadianism, and 9 borrowing. The state of Canadian dialectology, especially that of Newfoundland, is described with 11 examples. There is a bibliography of 21 entries, including 1 on place names.

158. Baker, R. J. "Linguistics and Literature in Canada." *CanL*, 1 (1959), 97-100.

This article points out that lexicology and dialectology aid the historian and the foreign critic of literature. It comments on the inadequacy of contemporary dictionaries for the study of CE and welcomes the start of work on *DCHP*.

159. Barkman, Bruce. Review of *The Winston Dictionary of Canadian English*. *Intermediate Edition*. *Ed. Thomas M. Paikeday*. *META: Journal des Traducteurs-Translators' Journal*, 17 (1972), 181-86.

The reviewer gives his doctrine of the purpose of school dictionaries. He praises *WI*'s pronunciation key, noting that it gives the CE pronunciation of *rot*, *wrought*, etc. He mentions *WI*'s spelling chart, its treatment of homographs, its preference for BE over AE spellings, and its spelling of inflections. He cites the complete entry for *fresh*, and discusses the dictionary's handling of Canadianisms and of technical terms.

160. Bateman, Stanley C.E. "Survey of Canadian English: A Comparison of the Language Patterns of English-Speaking New Brunswickers at Two Different Levels of Education." M.Ed. report. Univ. of New Brunswick, 1975.

This study is based on the responses of 149 freshman students at the University of New Brunswick to the SCE questionnaire. When the results were compared with those obtained in the original survey, 7 morphological and syntactical, 5 phonological, and 6 lexical items showed a difference of more than 20% from the figures obtained for the SCE. The changes showed the influence of extra schooling and of a wish for "correctness."

161. Bauerle, Richard F. "_Salties_ on the Great Lakes." _AS_, 45 (1970), 156-57.

This article notes that _saltie_ 'ocean-going vessel' is common in both CE and AE round the Great Lakes but that the meaning 'sailor on an ocean-going vessel' occurs only in CE.

162. Baugh, A.C. _A History of the English Language_. New York: Appleton-Century-Crofts, 1935. p. 397-98. 2nd ed. 1957. p. 388.

Both editions mention the shared history and the common circumstance of AE and CE, showing the strong influence of AE on CE. The first edition gives 2 examples of BE influence on CE; the second regards CE as a dialect of AE.

163. Belanger, John. "Where Is the Cache in the Snye?" _Maclean's Magazine_, 1 Jan. 1966, p. 47-48.

This notice of the then forthcoming _DCHP_ outlines its history and cites 12 Canadianisms, observing that many Canadianisms are loanwords and commenting on their semantic associations.

164. Beljaeva, T.M., and I.A. Potapova. _Anglijskij jazyk za predelam Anglii_. Leningrad: Gosydarstvennoe Ycheno-Pedagogicheskoe Isdatelstvo Ministerstva Prosveshchenia RSPhSP Leningradskoe Otdelenie, 1961. p. 46-51.

After a brief social and historical comment on Canada, this excerpt mentions 7 phonological features of CE, giving 16 examples. Various aspects of the CE vocabulary are discussed, with 70 supporting examples in roman script. Some of these seem slightly unusual, e.g., _bog-slad_, _merry-me-got_; the authors' only implied source for these is the periodical _Dialectal_ [sic] _Notes_. (The foregoing was prepared from a translation made by Miss Austra Reinvalds).

165. Bell, Inglis F. "Language." _CanL_, 3 (1960), 100.

This bibliographical checklist includes 6 items on CE. All are listed in other bibliographies.

166. ________. "Language." _CanL_, 7 (1961), 92.

This bibliographical checklist includes 2 items on CE, both listed in other bibliographies.

167. Belliveau, J.E. "Accent Indicates Caste." _Toronto Daily Star_, 17 May 1957, p. 25.

This article gives 2 lexical items stated to be typical of "U-English" in Canada. Then, claiming Walter S. Avis as its authority, the article cites 11 features of pronunciation, also said to be typical of a prestige dialect of CE.

168. ________. "Canadian Word Twists." _Toronto Daily Star_, 22 Oct. 1957, p. 21.

Reviewing a radio programme on Canadian dialects, the author claims distinctive speech for Manitoba and the west. The author also comments extensively on 8 of the differences which Walter S. Avis observed between Ontario and the U.S.

169. ________. "Chowder Pure Canadian." _Toronto Daily Star_, 10 May 1957, p. 33.

This article heralding _DCCD_ gives a brief description of its editors and shows the worth of _DCCD_ by citing 10 hitherto unrecognized Canadianisms.

Belliveau, J.E. Cont'd.

170. __________. "Do You Speak Good Canadian?" Star Weekly Magazine, 20 July 1957, p. 10-11 and 33.

Describing an early state of DCCD, this article emphasizes its uniqueness as an authority for both Canadian languages, separately and together. It gives 29 lexical Canadianisms and 1 phonological Canadianism that DCCD will define. A further 7 examples show CE borrowing from French. DCCD's functions are forecast, and the article includes notes on the personalities and methods behind it. An appendix entitled "How's Y-O-U-R Canadian?" gives 15 words whose CE pronunciation is unrecorded in any dictionary.

171. __________. "Need Folklore Glossary." Toronto Daily Star, 19 Mar. 1957, p. 21.

This article records 24 features of speech stated to be peculiar to particular, specified regions in Canada and laments their possible erasure by the mass media. It also gives 6 features stated to be Canadianisms.

172. Ben-Dor, Shmuel. Makkovik: Eskimos and Settlers in a Labrador Community: A Contrastive Study in Adaptation. Newfoundland Social and Economic Studies, 4. St. John's, Nfld.: Memorial Univ. of Newfoundland, 1966.

Some terms, technical and other, current in the speech of this community in eastern Labrador are cited and explained passim in this work. Many are placed in quotation marks.

173. Bengtsson, Elna. The Language and Vocabulary of Sam Slick. Upsala Canadian Studies, No. 5. Copenhagen: Munksgaard, 1956.

This work is mainly an extended comparison between the dialect of Sam Slick and the Northeastern dialect of AE. The chapter on phonology classifies its material under 45 ME phonological features. The chapter on grammar classifies its material under 8 parts of speech and 2 features of idiom. The conclusion states that "Sam's speech was a correct imitation of the language in the rural districts of the North East" (p. 41). There is an addendum on "Titbits of American Lingo."

174. Bennett, Wilf. "Red-Eye in Bennett buggy?" _Province_ (Vancouver), 23 Aug. 1967, sec. 3, p. 23.

This report of a paper read by M.H. Scargill in Vancouver in 1967 looks forward to the publication of _DCHP_ and gives and illustrates 5 sources of Canadianisms.

175. Berton, Pierre. "Explaining and Expanding My Own Canadian Glossary." _Toronto Daily Star_, 31 Oct. 1962, p. 37.

This article justifies as Canadianisms 13 of the items in "A Glossary of Distinctive Canadian Terms" by the same author, q.v. It adds 12 items, rejects 4 suggestions, characterizes a further 18 as debatable, and ends by defining 7 of the items included in the original.

176. ________. "A Glossary of Distinctive Canadian Terms." _Toronto Daily Star_, 23 Oct. 1962, p. 17.

This article records 49 distinctively Canadian items stated to have passed into general use and a further 63 that are not readily understood but that "most literate Canadians ought to comprehend."

177. Bird, Barbara. "Lumbering Was Rough and Ready in 18th Century New Brunswick." _Daily Gleaner_ (Fredericton), 17 May 1975, p. 5.

This article includes the legend that the origin of the expression _the main John_ lies in a description of John Glazier as _the mean John_ by an Irish-English speaker who pronounced _mean_ as _main_.

178. Bloomfield, Morton W. "Canadian English and its Relation to Eighteenth Century American Speech." _JEGP_. 47 (1948), 59-67. Reprinted in "Readings on Language in Canada." Ed. Ronald H. Southerland (q.v.). 19-33. Reprinted in _Canadian English: Origins and Structures_. Ed. J.K. Chambers (q.v.). p. 1-11.

After an outline history of CE, the author examines 9 phonological features (17 examples), 3 syntactical features, and 10 lexical examples from CE. These, together with observations from record #67 (See "American Speech Records" by H.M. Ayres and H.C. Greet) suggest that CE is part of General American. Maritime speech, where distinctive, reflects New England influence; it should thus illuminate the history of eighteenth-century AE. An appendix contains phonetic transcriptions by J.S. Kenyon of 44 words spoken by informants from Halifax, N.S., Montreal, Ontario, and Saskatchewan.

179. Booth, A.D. "Canadian Words." Star-Phoenix (Saskatoon), 14 Feb. 1968, p. 24.

This review of DCHP notes the large number of Canadianisms therein and comments on their historical interest, remarking also on the inclusion of up-to-date technical words and commending DCHP's illustrations.

180. The British Council. Varieties of English: American, Canadian, Australian, New Zealand. Specialised Bibliography. London: The British Council, 1973.

In this work, the section on bibliographies lists item 103 of this Bibliography. The section on Canadian English lists items 152, 153, 280, 484, and 621 of this Bibliography.

181. Brook, G.L. "Canada," in English Dialects. 2nd ed. London: Andre Deutsch, 1965. p. 127-28.

The author emphasizes the importance of Loyalist and British influence on the formation of CE, but notes also the strong influence of AE. He forecasts that CE will become more like AE and cites the state of our knowledge of 4 lexical and 4 phonological items to show the need for further research on CE.

182. Brooke, Rupert. Letters from America. New York: Charles Scribner's Sons, 1916.

This writer mentions "the soft Canadian accent" (p. 57). He alleges that CE prefers bunch over crowd, characterizing this as "the one distinction between the Canadian and American languages" (p. 76). He uses the quasi-phonetic spelling "T'ranto" to show the local pronunciation of Toronto (p. 79).

183. Brown, Miriam Williams. "The Canadian Speech: A Criticism." Canadian Magazine, 36 (Nov. 1910-Apr. 1911), 292-94.

The writer accuses Canadians of speaking indistinctly and with a "nasal twang," and uses quasi-phonetic spelling to indicate examples in 2 sentences, 1 phrase, and 12 words.

She refers to Canadians pronouncing taught as "tot" and Toronto as "Trntuh."

184. Brown, Thomas Kite, and Henry Alexander, eds. Winston Simplified Dictionary for Canadian Schools. Toronto: The John C. Winston Co., 1937.

According to its preface, this dictionary has a vocabulary of about 32,500 words, including 15,100 main entries, and gives 1,100 illustrations. The front matter describes the dictionary's treatment of parts of speech, labelling, variant spellings, derivatives, homographs, and foreign words. There is a section on the spelling and pronunciation of inflected forms, and there is a key to the dictionary's phonetic script. There is little that is specially Canadian about the book.

185. Brunner, K. Die Englische Sprache. Bd. I. Tübingen: Niemeyer, 1960. Bd. II. 1962.

The author comments (p. 216-18) that CE is influenced by both BE and AE; influence from BE has inhibited the spread of some American expressions, of which 2 examples are given. The pronunciation of CE in general resembles that of AE.

186. Buckler, Ernest. "As the Saying Went, or Slugs and Guts," in Oxbells and Fireflies. Toronto: McClelland and Stewart, 1968. p. 160-68.

This item gives and, where the meaning is not obvious, defines 109 Nova Scotia words, idioms, and sayings.

187. Bursill-Hall, G.L. "How Canadians Speak." CanL, 50 (1971), 69-72.

This review of Speaking Canadian English by Mark M. Orkin, q.v., comments on Orkin's elegant style and considerable research. It mentions unfavorably his uncertainty in the use of some technical terms, giving 2 illustrations of this, and sees a lack of "theoretical sophistication," especially in regard to syntax. His failure to state criteria leads the reader to think that all Canadians speak Ontario English. The review finally pleads for more study of CE, especially in universities.

188. C., G.H. "On Pronunciation in Particular and Sticking One's Chin Out in General." Leader-Post (Regina), 28 Nov. 1939, p. 4.

This article describes the varieties of pronunciation of respite and ensign in CE.

189. Cameron, Agnes Deans. "New Words with Crops of Yellow Wheat." Canadian Magazine of Politics, Science, Art and Literature, 31 (May-Oct. 1908), 141-43.

This article enshrines 30 examples of western Canadian slang in a fictitious account of the trials of a cheechako.

190. Campbell, A. Luella. "Vowel Shortening and T-Voicing in Canadian English." CWPL, 1:1 (1975), 26-28.

This paper discusses the absence of shortened vowels before voiceless consonants and of the voicing of intervocalic /t/ from the idiolect of a speaker from southern Ontario. These characteristics are related to the speaker's profession of teaching.

191. Caramazza, A., G.H. Yeni-Komshian, E.B. Zurif, and E. Carbone. "The acquisition of a new phonological contrast: The case of stop consonants in French-English bilinguals." JAS, 54 (1973), 421-28.

As part of the experiment described herein, 10 unilingual speakers of CE each spoke 3 words for each of the phoneme sequences /pa/, /ba/, /ta/, /da/, /ka/, /ga/. The same group of informants also categorized as containing either a voiced or a voiceless stop 37 artificially produced syllables for each of the pairs /p/ and /b/, /t/ and /d/, and /k/ and /g/. On the basis of instrumental measurement, the authors concluded that voice onset time is an important cue for separating homorganic initial stops into phonemic categories.

192. Cartwright, George. "Glossary," in Journal of Transactions and Events During a Residence of Nearly Sixteen Years on the Coast of Labrador. Newark (England): Allin and Ridge, 1792. I, ix-xvi; II, iii-x; III, iii-x.

This glossary gives 134 lexical items observed by the author in Labrador. (The glossary is printed three times, once in each volume of the work).

193. Cartwright, H.L. "What's in a Name?" Times (London), Supplement on Canada. 30 Nov. 1959, p. ix.

This article describes the difference between the BE and the CE meanings of the title Queen's Counsel.

194. Chamberlain, A.F. "Algonkian Words in American English." JAF, 15 (1902), 240-67.

This article lists 137 words of Amerindian origin in the English language, including 14 specifically stated to be in use in the English of various regions of Canada.

195. ________. "Dialect Research in Canada." DN, 1 (1890), 45-56.

After noticing the amount of research then still to be done on CE, this article lists: 20 lexical items from Peterborough, Ont., and another 8 observed among younger speakers in the same place; 4 observed both in Peterborough and in Toronto; 1 in Toronto; 4 in the Hudson Bay area; 9 common throughout Canada; 3 from older English dialects. Another 16 items, common to Peterborough and Toronto, are given in phonetic script, and an Appendix lists 3 articles on CE.

196. ________. "Etymology of 'Caribou.'" AA, 3 (1901), 587-88.

This article records the word caribou from Nova Scotia and New Brunswick.

197. ________. "Memorials of the 'Indian.'" JAF, 15 (1902), 107-16.

This article records 1 plant name from Newfoundland, and 2 from Newfoundland and Labrador, all incorporating the word Indian.

198. Chambers, E.T.D. "The Philology of the Ouananiche: A Plea for the Recognition of Priority of Nomenclature." PTRSC, 2nd Series, Vol. 2 (1896), Sec. II, p. 131-39.

This article gives 27 different spellings of the word ouananiche, and adds the provenance of 25 of these forms. The identity of the fish is discussed at length, a more correct definition of it is provided, and the spelling ouananiche is preferred.

The etymology of the word is given. The namaycush and the muskellunge are also mentioned.

199. Chambers, J.K. "Canadian Raising." CJL, 18 (1973), 113-35. Reprinted in Canadian English: Origins and Structures. Ed. J.K. Chambers (q.v.). p. 83-100.

The author cautions that "Canadian Raising," which is the name for the high onset of the diphthongs /ay/ and /aw/, is not limited to Canada and that for this study he has used only 10 informants, all from Ontario. Viewing the Canadian /ay/ as the raising of an earlier [ay], he states a provisional rule and relates it to rules for voicing and shortening. Raised forms have been generalized because the rule has been reordered from "low level" to "high level." Further evidence permits the full statement of the rule. Canadian Raising has now attained "linguistic stability."

200. __________. "The Ottawa Valley 'twang,'" in Canadian English: Origins and Structures. Ed. J.K. Chambers (q.v.). p. 55-59.

The writer notes that there are at least 2 Ottawa Valley dialects, phonologically distinct. The first has a raised onset of /ay/ in some contexts only (3 examples) and of /aw/ in all contexts (6 examples). The second has a low front onset of /ay/ (3 examples) and /aw/ (8 examples), and has only low front vowels before /r/ (4 examples).

201. __________. Review of Regional Language Studies ... Newfoundland. Ed. William J. Kirwin. CJL, 20 (1975), 233.

This review of Nos. 1 through 4 of RLS picks out some articles therein of use to dialectologists.

202. __________, ed. Canadian English: Origins and Structures. Toronto: Methuen, 1975.

This anthology contains items 010, 130, 141, 178, 199, 200, 263, 306, 314, 347, 397, 489, 558, 567, 590, 623, and 660 of this Bibliography. Some are slightly revised. There is a brief introduction, and throughout the book there are half-page comments on the articles.

203. Chaplain, The (pseudonym). "Shaganappi." Canadian Magazine of Politics, Science, Art and Literature, 27 (May-Oct. 1906), 285-86.

This article includes a poem on shaganippi, showing some of the many meanings of this word.

204. Chicanot, E.L. "The Polyglot Vernacular of the Canadian Northwest." MLR, 10 (1915), 88-89.

This article records 8 loanwords from Indian languages and 2 semantic Indianisms in use in the Canadian Northwest. Loanwords from Gaelic, though mentioned, are unexemplified. The article also observes 8 loanwords from "Mexican" and 8 from French.

205. Chiu, Rosaline K. "Register Constraints on the Choice of the English Verb." EngQ, 6 (1973), 123-37.

After describing the corpus (the English used by public servants in Canada) and the method of analysing it, the author concludes that English-speaking public servants in Canada use one quite limited set of verbs in writing and another quite limited set for speech: the 30 most popular verbs from each mode are cited. The frequency of the verbs from this corpus is then compared to their frequency in other corpuses. Finally, the author concludes that the sets of linguistic structures in which these verbs appear are also limited.

206. Chorny, M. Review of Looking at Language. Ed. M.H. Scargill and P.G. Penner. CJL, 13 (1967), 59-60.

This review outlines the contents of Looking at Language and comments on how well it achieves its authors' purpose.

207. Clapin, Sylva. New Dictionary of Americanisms. New York: Louis Weiss [c. 1902]. Reprinted Detroit: Gale Research, 1968.

On the basis of an examination of the entries under A, B, and C, it is estimated that this dictionary contains about 200 entries attributed to CE.

208. Collett, Maxwell. "The Harbour Buffett Motor Boat." Newfoundland Quarterly, 67:2 (July 1969), 15-20.

After illustrating their use in the description of how a boat is built, this article lists and defines 110 boat-building words used in Newfoundland; some have slightly localized senses.

209. Colombo, John Robert, ed. Colombo's Canadian Quotations. Edmonton: Hurtig Publishers, 1974.

There are quotations relating to CE on p. 9a, 10a, 51b, 77b, 150b, 240b, 300a, 341b, 456a (2), 466a, 476a, 483b, 509a, 524b, 554a, 635a-b, and 649a.

210. [Cooper, John A.] "Editorial Comment." Canadian Magazine of Politics, Science, Art and Literature, 13 (May-Oct. 1899), 481-82.

This article debates the spelling of the preposition in coureurs de(s) bois, giving reasons for both spellings.

211. Cotter, H.M.S. "A Fur Trade Glossary." Beaver, No. 272 (Sept. 1941), p. 36-39.

This article records 179 words of various origins observed at several Hudson's Bay Company trading posts.

212. Courteville, Yves. "Syntagmatique des titres de journeaux anglais." M.A. thesis. Univ. de Montréal, 1957.

Though based mainly on data from British newspapers, this study includes material from the Montreal Gazette and the Montreal Star. It concludes that the principal syntactic feature of titles and headings in the English press is ellipsis, often carried to the point of ambiguity.

213. Creighton, Helen. Folklore of Lunenburg County, Nova Scotia. National Museum of Canada Bulletin No. 117. Anthropological Series No. 29. Ottawa: King's Printer, 1950. p. 105-14.

This records 51 proverbs, 157 sayings, idioms, and other lexical items, 3 syntactical, 2 morphological, and 3 phonetic items observed by the author in or near Lunenburg County, N.S. For all but 10, the name of the community of observation is given.

214. Crofton, F. Blake. "Our Fighting Vocabulary." Canadian Magazine of Politics, Science, Art and Literature, 17 (May-Oct. 1901), 52-54.

This article records 4 CE slang words for 'to beat (someone),' including 1 from "Sam Slick."

215. Crone, Kennedy. British Spelling of English as the Canadian National Standard. Montreal: Canadian Geographical Society [c. 1931].

The author characterizes Canadian spelling as an unsystematic mixture of British and American practices and gives 28 examples of Canadian adoptions of American spellings. This mixture does not in itself constitute a standard. He argues for the adoption of the British system.

216. Cronin, Fergus. "Do You Speak Canadian?" Canadian Weekly: Star Weekly Magazine (Toronto), 27 Feb.-5 Mar. 1965, p. 16-17.

After citing 20 Canadian lexical items contrastive with American usage, 3 with British, 13 general Canadianisms, and 19 regionalisms, this article reports Walter S. Avis's doctrine that English is Canadian "wherever it differs from the English spoken in either England or the United States." It then gives Avis's criteria for Canadianisms, citing 16 examples. The article notes that linguistic change renders dictionaries obsolete, as 7 examples show. The lexicographical work of Avis and of M.H. Scargill is also described.

217. [Crowe, Gordon.] "Bluenose Conversion." Valley Views (Musquodoboit, N.S., Rural Development Board), No. 32 (6 Aug. 1975), p. 2.

This article records 12 lexical items and 2 idioms said to be common in the speech of the Musquodoboit Valley.

218. Cullen, Constance. "Dialect Research on Prince Edward Island." EngQ, 4:3 (Fall 1971), 51-53.

This article reports some of the results from a questionnaire sent to the P.E.I. communities of: Kinkora, mainly Irish in origin; Post Hill, mainly English; North Rustico, formerly francophone; and Belfast, originally Scottish. The words snool, thra, clart, and foother were known in Kinkora alone, and <u>fooster</u> was known in Kinkora mainly; <u>ceilidh</u> was known in all 4 communities, but most widely in Belfast; <u>time</u> was universally known, but in an unusually wide sense.

219. Currell, Harvey. "Now, the Canadians have a word for it." <u>Telegram</u> (Toronto), 17 June 1967, p. 23.

This article gives a short history of DCE, and a summary of its volume titles. It notes the <u>Telegram</u>'s adoption of <u>SD</u> as its spelling standard and comments on <u>SD</u>'s spelling practice. A few of <u>SD</u>'s lexical items are cited.

220. D., J. "Jottings." <u>AS</u>, 7 (1931), 232.

This records the word <u>furnovated</u> in the slogan of a firm of furriers in Montreal.

221. Darbelnet, Jean. "Accent de phrase et dialectique en anglais et en français," in <u>Interlinguistica: Sprachvergleich und Übersetzung</u>. Festschrift zum 60. Geburtstag von Mario Wandruszka. Ed. Karl-Richard Bausch and Hans-Martin Gauger. Tübingen: Niemeyer, 1971. p. 416-24

This article discusses the different methods used by English and French respectively to accent one particular word from a sentence or a phrase. Canadian publications are the source of 12 examples, but in 5 of these the author is American.

222. Darnell, Regna, ed. <u>Linguistic Diversity in Canadian Society</u>. Edmonton: Linguistic Research, 1971.

This anthology contains items 265, 617, and 618 of this <u>Bibliography</u>.

223. Dashwood-Jones, D. Review of <u>The Senior Dictionary</u>. Ed. Walter S. Avis and others. <u>CJL</u>, 13 (1967), 57-58.

This review outlines the criteria of word-selection used in <u>SD</u> and notes that in six months of referring all suitable queries to it, the author failed only thrice to find an answer.

224. Daviault, Pierre. "L'élément canadien-français de l'anglais d'Amérique." PTRSC, 3rd Series, Vol. 46 (1952), Sec. I, p. 5-18.

This article cites 20 geographical words, including 9 compounds, 10 general words, 5 words of Creole origin, and 1 from Chinook Jargon, all of them loans from French into NAE. However, it does not distinguish between currency in AE and in CE.

225. ________. "The Evolution of the English and French Languages in Canada." PTRSC, 3rd Series, Vol. 53 (1959), Minutes, p. 63-72.

This article points out that the languages of Canada are new varieties of English and French, and instances, for CE, its spelling and pronunciation. The Canadian languages differ from their sources because migrant languages are simultaneously archaizing and neologizing. Their speakers' histories have affected them, as has the linguistic inventiveness of Canadians, of which 2 examples are given. Only those changes which are produced by ignorance, indifference, or thoughtlessness are to be rejected.

226. ________. "Français et anglais du Canada," in Studia Varia: Royal Society of Canada, Literary and Scientific Papers. Ed. E.G.D. Murray. Toronto: Univ. of Toronto for the Royal Society of Canada, 1957. p. 3-9.

The things which made CE a "new" language are the Canadian preservation in politics, government, etc., of terms forgotten in the U.S., and the author instances Canadian inventiveness here. The individuality of the Canadian lexicon is exemplified by 3 loanwords from Amerindian languages, 16 from French, and 5 from divers sources, as also by 19 word creations.

227. Davidson, Rev. J.A. "Canadiana." United Church Observer, 1 Oct. 1969, p. 29-30.

This review of DCHP quotes Walter S. Avis's description of CE as "neither American nor British, but a complex different in many respects from both." It characterizes DCHP as "an indispensable reference book for . . . Canadian studies." It cites 3 words from DCHP and suggests 2 which it might have included.

Davidson, Rev. J.A. Cont'd

228. ________. "Speaking Canajan." Globe and Mail (Toronto), 3 July 1974, p. 29.

This review of Canajan, Eh? by Mark M. Orkin, q.v., describes the book as amusing but suggests that much allegedly "Canajan" pronunciation is merely the result of slurring in rapid speech. The extensive use of "Canajan" in both Ottawa and Saskatchewan is denied. The reviewer gives alternatives to the pronunciation of Saskatchewan described by Orkin.

229. ________. [pseud. "John MacDade."] "Our very own sounds." Globe Magazine, 27 Sept. 1969, p. 13-15.

This is mainly a rearrangement of "What's This about a Canadian Accent?" by the same author, q.v.

230. ________. [pseud. "John McDade."] "What's This about a Canadian Accent?" Canadian Weekly: Star Weekly Magazine, 12-18 Jan. 1963, p. 2, 3 and 15.

This article describes, in non-technical language, 3 features of pronunciation which allegedly differentiate CE from AE: the CE treatment of /r/, of some vowels, and of /t/; and it exemplifies the last 2 features. It then discusses regional dialects across Canada, drawing attention to historical survivals therein. Finally, the article forecasts the continuance of CE in a form different from that of AE.

231. Davies, D.L. Glossary and Handbook of Canadian--British Words. Vancouver: n. p., 1967. [Available from Pauline's Books, Vancouver.]

This handbook contains 850 entries, listing 1,170 words and phrases. They are claimed to be the major differences between everyday CE and BE and are explained in BE.

232. Davis, Alva L., and Lawrence M. Davis. "Recordings of Standard English." NADS, 1:3 (Nov. 1969), 4-17.

This article reports that the project described possesses recorded tapes from St. John's, Nfld., Halifax, N.S., Saint John, N.B., Toronto, Winnipeg, and Vancouver. It also gives the questionnaire followed in making the tapes.

Davis, Alva L. Cont'd.

233. __________, and Raven I. McDavid, Jr. "'Shivaree': An Example of Cultural Diffusion." AS, 24 (1949), 249-55.

Based on data from LAUSC and from that collected by Henry Alexander in the Maritimes, this study shows shivaree to be common through eastern Canada. The alternative, salute, is shown from Nova Scotia.

234. __________, __________, and Virginia Glenn McDavid, eds. A Compilation of the Work Sheets of the Linguistic Atlas of the United States and Canada and Associated Projects. 2nd ed. Chicago: Univ. of Chicago, 1969.

This compilation includes some of the material from some of the questionnaires used for surveys in Canada.

235. Deacon, William Arthur. "Need Canadian Dictionary." Globe and Mail (Toronto), 23 Aug. 1958, p. 9.

After quoting the statement of the need for a Canadian dictionary as made in "Canadian English Merits a Dictionary" by Walter S. Avis, q.v., this article cites 23 Canadianisms in support of this. It also mentions the increase in the Canadian lexicon represented by the accession of Newfoundland and continued by Canadian linguistic inventiveness.

236. Dean, Christopher. "Is There a Distinctive Literary Canadian English?" AS, 38 (1963), 278-82.

From a study of some Canadian stories, the author finds, in 154 pages which he read, only 52 words and constructions which a Britisher would regard as non-British. However, since only 2 of these are recognizably Canadian, he concludes that, within its limits, his study shows that there is no distinctive literary Canadian English.

237. Dear, Ruth. "Some Queries about Regionalisms." AS, 35 (1960), 298-300.

This article inquires about the geographical spread of magazine 'general storehouse or silo,' recorded in Canada; of corn boil 'festive gathering to boil and eat green corn,' recorded in Garson, Ont.; and of chop 'whole ground grain,' recorded in Calgary.

238. Dent, Percy. "From Chechaco to Sour-dough." Chambers's Journal, 7th Series, No. 12, 7 Jan. 1922, p. 90-91.

This article notes that, in the Klondike region of the Yukon, the word "Chechaco (che-chaw-ker)" is applied to a newcomer until he has seen the ice "come and go." Thereafter, he is a "sour-dough."

239. Devine, P.K. Folklore of Newfoundland in Old Words, Phrases, and Expressions. St. John's, Nfld.: Robinson, 1937.

This work includes a glossary of 962 entries, each defining a word or phrase in use in Newfoundland. A further 18 phrases are glossed under the heading "Dialect," 25 under "Proverbs and Sayings," and 51 under "Some Expressive Terms."

240. Dickson, L.M. "What Language?" Canadian Bookman, No. 16 (Jan. 1934), p. 6-7.

After outlining the sources of many Americanisms, this article lists 40 Americanisms in CE. A further 8 are noted as being derived from Amerindian languages, 7 from Spanish, and 11 from other languages. Pioneer life, railroading, and sport have contributed 9, 14, and 2 respectively. The result of this American influence is to hybridize CE.

241. Dillard, Joey Lee. All-American English: A History of the English Language in America. New York: Random House, 1975.

On p. 28-29, the author gives 8 quotations from CE of 1741 to c1791, claiming that they show the occurrence in Canada of a branch of a pidgin English of world-wide distribution.

242. __________. "The History of Black English in Nova Scotia--A First Step." AfrLRev, 9 (1970-1971), 263-79.

The author claims that Black English in Nova Scotia originates in a pidgin once common in West Africa, America, and the West Indies. Literary evidence dating the Black English of Nova Scotia back to the mid-eighteenth century shows it to be structurally similar in 7 characteristics to this pidgin. Some speakers of Nova Scotia Black English have retained these characteristics, while others have developed a decreolized sociolect approximating Standard English.

243. Dillon, Virginia. "The Anglo-Irish Element in the Speech of the Southern Shore of Newfoundland." M.A. thesis. Memorial Univ. of Newfoundland, 1968.

After discussing the criteria for "Irishness," the author characterizes the words in the glossary in this work as concerning religion, household and agriculture, or personal relationships, and she points out that changes are overtaking these words. The glossary contains 233 entries, each giving authentic, located citations for the word glossed.

244. Doering, John Frederick, and Eileen Elita Doering. "Some Western Ontario Folk Beliefs and Practices." JAF, 51 (1938), 60-68.

This article records 51 "provincialisms, unusual meanings of words, etc.," chiefly from Huron, Perth, Waterloo, Wellington, and Brant Counties in Ontario. Some examples are given in quasi-phonetic spelling.

245. Donahue, Bob. "From Bennett Buggy to Ogopogo This Love Affair Has Ten Years." Victoria Daily Times (Victoria, B.C.), 7 Dec. 1965, p. 20.

This account of a paper by M.H. Scargill on the then in preparation DCHP points out that it will have implications for history, geography, and sociology; 14 words and phrases are cited to prove this. A further 15 examples illustrate regionalisms and nicknames and show the dictionary's importance as comment on civilization in general.

246. Doody, M.R. Letter to the editor. Globe and Mail (Toronto), 15 May 1974, p. 6.

This writer objects to the over-use by members of the Women's Liberation movement of the word chauvinism.

247. Doole, Bill. "His Chesterfield Didn't Have Filter." Daily Times (Brantford, Ont.), 14 July 1967, p. 3.

This is mainly a reproduction of "Canadian English" by Walter S. Avis, in SD, q.v.

248. Dowell, John. "Canadian English." Kingston Whig-Standard, 15 Apr. 1967, p. 17.

This report of an interview with Walter S. Avis points out that SD, then in preparation, will be based in usage and will show the Canadian spellings and meanings of words. The article includes 1 example of the Canadian spelling dilemma and 5 of lexical Canadianisms.

249. Drysdale, P.D. "Dictionaries for the Schools." Education (Toronto), 4 (1962), 105-19.

Having outlined the principles and procedures underlying a good, modern, descriptive dictionary, this article shows their applicability to Canadian lexicography in general and argues their special applicability to school dictionaries.

250. ________. "A First Approach to Newfoundland Phonemics." JCLA, 5 (1959), 25-34.

After a detailed description of the origins of the dialect pattern of modern Newfoundland, including the hypothesizing of 5 or even 6 dialect areas for the island, the article describes the phonemics of Conception Bay dialect. Of its consonants, only 4 differ significantly from those of NAE. The dialect has 10 vowel phonemes and 11 falling-diphthong phonemes. All are discussed, the vowel phonemes being exemplified as well.

251. ________. "Her Parkee Made of Caribou: Using a Dictionary as a Sourcebook." EngQ, 4:3 (Fall 1971), 47-50.

This article shows how the semantic field traceable from DCHP's cross-references under atigi exemplifies borrowing and shows its historical significance and the linguistic behaviour of loanwords. The semantic field round the word caribou shows how a language can deal with the unfamiliar, while ski-doo exemplifies the process of word creation.

252. ________. "Why a High-School Dictionary?" Speaking of Dictionaries, No. 2. Toronto: Gage (Nov. 1966), p. 1-4.

This gives the qualities of a good high-school dictionary, including the need for references to Canadian life in a dictionary for Canadians.

Drysdale, P.D. Cont'd.

253. __________, W.F. Mackey, M.H. Scargill, and J.-P. Vinay. "Pitch and Stress as Phonemes: Analysis or Synthesis?" JCLA, 4 (1958), 61-62.

Though primarily theoretical, this article argues that in some localities CE has only 3 pitch and 3 stress phonemes.

254. Dudek, Louis. "Is There A Canadian Language? Depends What You Mean by 'Language.'" Gazette (Montreal), 22 Apr. 1967, p. 20.

The writer gives some statistics on the DCE series. He then compares Canadian lexicography with American and comments, giving examples, on the value of a dictionary which mirrors Canadian culture in being neither British nor American.

255. __________. "Some Great Christmas Gift Suggestions From The Centennial Book Bag." Gazette (Montreal), 9 Dec. 1967, p. 28.

This article notes the usefulness of DCHP's lexicon as an index of Canadian culture. It suggests some additional sources of Canadianisms and adds that some items claimed to be Canadianisms may not in fact be such.

256. Duffus, Maureen. "Living History in a Dictionary." Daily Colonist (Victoria, B.C.), 23 Jan. 1966, p. 18.

This article on an early stage of DCHP cites 6 Canadianisms to show how lexicography leads to an interest in past Canadian culture. It also briefly pictures a lexicographer at work.

257. Dunbabin, Thomas. "Canada's Own Dictionary Is Coming." London Free Press, 12 Feb. 1957, p. 4.

This article on an early stage of DCE sees two principal dialect areas in Canada: Mainland and Newfoundland, of which it cites 3 examples. It uses 3 examples to show Canada's preservation of words archaic elsewhere and 2 examples to show CE agreeing with AE and differing from BE, as also to show dialect differentiation within Canada. The function of a dictionary in possibly determining Canadian spelling is also mentioned.

258. Dunlap, A.R. "Observations on American Colloquial Idiom." _AS_, 20 (1945), 12-21.

This article notes the occurrence of affirmative _anymore_ from Cobourg, Ont., and of _happen you_ from Truro, N.S., which area the author thinks to be the centre of currency of this idiom. Calgary and Cobourg are said not to use _like for_ to replace _like_ (vb.). Calgary uses _off of_, but not _off from_, and Cobourg rejects both.

259. Dunlop, W.J. "Do Canadians Speak English?" _Univ. of Toronto Monthly_, No. 35 (Feb. 1935), p. 128-29.

The author accuses Canadians of being "lip-lazy " and of saying _whut_, _wuz_, _fur_, _nut_, and _ut_, for _what_, _was_, _for_, _not_, and _it_.

260. Dunraven, Rt. Hon. the Earl of. "Moose-hunting in Canada." _Nineteenth Century_, 6 (1879), 45-65.

This article includes a list of 12 loanwords borrowed from French and Spanish and current in CE. An illustrative phrase shows the meaning of each word.

261. Eggleston, Wilfrid. "On Chowder and Other Word Origins." _Ottawa Journal_, 18 Oct. 1969, p. 44.

This article traces the Canadian word _chowder_ to its origin in French and suggests how it may have been borrowed. (Other words mentioned in this article are not specifically Canadian.)

262. Elliott, John K. "Study of Canadian terms." _London Free Press_, 6 July 1968, p. 7-M.

This review of _DCHP_ outlines its history and remarks on and exemplifies its provision of a historical record of Canadianisms through dated quotations. _DCHP_'s criteria for Canadianisms are summarized. The first and last entries in _DCHP_ are noted, and the divers origins of Canadianisms are mentioned, 3 examples thereof being given.

263. Emeneau, M.B. "The Dialect of Lunenburg, Nova Scotia." Language, 11 (1935), 140-47. Reprinted in Canadian English: Origins and Structures. Ed. J.K. Chambers (q.v.). p. 34-39.

The author first summarizes the history of the area, showing its German element to be predominantly Palatinate. In phonology, the allophones of /aʊ/ and /aɪ/ are discussed, with 28 examples, and the loss of preconsonantal /r/ with 55; this last may show German influence. The ways of anglicizing German personal names are shown in 22 examples. German influence is seen in 2 syntactical features (10 examples) and in 7 idioms and 15 lexical examples.

264. __________. "A Further Note on the Dialect of Lunenburg, Nova Scotia." Language, 16 (1940), 214-15.

The survival of belsnickel (pl. belsnickels) as a term for a Christmas mummer provides further evidence of the Palatine origin of Lunenburg's German-descended inhabitants.

265. Emery, George. "Negro English in Amber Valley, Alberta," in Linguistic Diversity in Canadian Society. Ed. Regna Darnell (q.v.). p. 45-59.

The author holds that linguistic investigation must study a community's communicative habits as a whole. He exemplifies the survival in Amber Valley Negro English of an archaic word form, and gives 3 examples of the use of language as an avoidance technique. He gives 6 examples of the effects of local culture on the local dialect and 2 of the influence of American Black English. The speech of the informants is recorded mainly in quasi-phonetic spelling.

266. England, George Allan. "Glossary of Commonly Used Newfoundland Words and Phrases," in Vikings of the Ice. New York: Doubleday, Page, 1924. p. 311-23.

This Glossary lists 930 words and phrases observed by the author in Newfoundland. Of the entries, 206 are quasi-phonetic spellings, presumably to represent Newfoundland pronunciation of words in common use.

267. __________. "Newfoundland Dialect Items." DN, 5 (1925), 322-46.

Based on the author's observations during visits to Newfoundland in 1920 and 1922, this article gives a brief introduction, quoting 19 Newfoundlandisms. The rest of the article is a glossary of 932 entries. Phonological information in phonetic or quasi-phonetic script is included for 66 entries. Morphemic information is included for 15. There are definitions for 1,002 items. The author suggests 26 possible etymologies, and there are comments on usage for 8 items. There are 120 illustrations, some in quotation marks.

268. English, L.E.F. Historic Newfoundland. St. John's, Nfld.: Newfoundland and Labrador Tourist Development Office [1955] rev. 1968. p. 29-31 and 34-35. 2nd ed. 1969. p. 29-33.

After a note on the dialectal diversity of Newfoundland, this work gives a glossary of 176 lexical items, "culled from a collection gathered from every part of the province " and in quasi-phonetic spelling. Next is a list of 57 Newfoundland sayings and, finally, another of 54 figures of speech.

269. Evans, Mary S. "Terms from the Labrador Coast." AS, 6 (1930), 56-58.

This article records 1 morphemic and 32 lexical items, including 7 terms of endearment, recorded by the author in Fox Harbor, Labrador, in 1926. The author notes that 11 of these occur in the Journal of Transactions and Events During A Residence of Nearly Sixteen Years on the Coast of Labrador by George Cartwright, q.v. The pronunciation of keg as "kag" is also noted.

270. Falconer, Sir Robert A. The United States as a Neighbour. Cambridge: Cambridge Univ., 1925. p. 203-04.

The author remarks that the speech of much of Ontario is derived from Pennsylvania or western New York and differs from the speech of the Maritimes, which the author holds to be derived from that of New England. However, despite its continuing affinity with AE, CE has drawn much from BE.

271. Faris, James C. Cat Harbour: A Newfoundland Fishing Settlement. Newfoundland Social and Economic Studies, No. 3. Toronto: Univ. of Toronto for Memorial Univ. of Newfoundland, 1972.

Many terms, technical and otherwise, current in the speech of the community studied are cited and explained in this book. The author notes (p. x) that "Words, phrases, idioms, and sentences in single quotation marks are of Cat Harbour usage."

Faris, James C. Cont'd.

272. __________. "The Dynamics of Verbal Exchange: A Newfoundland Example." _Anthropologica_, N.S. 8 (1966), 235-48.

This article, based on the author's personal observation in Cat Harbour, Nfld., records and marks in single quotation marks 25 local words and phrases.

273. Ferguson, D.W. "'Any More.'" _AS_, 7 (1932), 233-34.

This reports the use of affirmative _any more_ in southwestern Ontario.

274. Fetherling, Doug. "Even when we swear we're all colonials." _SatN_, May 1971, p. 34-35.

The author humorously laments Canadians' lack of linguistic originality, especially in obscenity, slang, eponyms, and figures of speech. He offers 8 original creations intended to better the situation.

275. __________. "Speak American or speak English: a choice of imperialisms." _SatN_, Sept. 1970, p. 33-34.

This article points out that CE is a blend of AE and BE. It quotes 3 examples of American influence from technology and 3 (of spelling) from Canadian style-manuals. It also quotes 3 examples of BE spellings, with 2 more from style manuals. It gives 2 examples of the CBC's retention of BE pronunciations.

276. Finnigan, Joan. "Only Canada has beer parlors." _Canadian Magazine_, 28 Jan.-4 Feb. 1967, p. 7.

This advance notice of _DCHP_ cites 11 Canadianisms as examples of what will appear in the dictionary; 4 more illustrate the linguistic borrowing which distinguishes CE; and another 10 show the lexical contribution of Canadian politics and social life. The last 4 examples quoted reflect distinctively Canadian foods and drinks. The article ends with M.H. Scargill's view that "the existence of Canadian English is proof of an emerging culture."

277. Firestone, Melvin M. _Brothers and Rivals: Patrilocality in Savage Cove_. Newfoundland Social and Economic Studies, No. 5. St. John's, Nfld.: Memorial Univ. of Newfoundland, 1967.

Many terms, technical and otherwise, current in the speech of the community studied are cited and explained _passim_ in this book. Many are italicized or placed in quotation marks; the pronunciation of some is indicated in quasi-phonetic spelling.

278. Fisher, John. "English by Radio," in _Personality, Appearance and Speech_ by T.H. Pear. London: Allen and Unwin, 1957. p. 104-05.

This report of a radio broadcast by the author in 1948 claims that all Canadians speak more or less alike. Canadian pronunciations are said to derive from BE, occasional foreign influence being exemplified from syntax. Canadian "short or thin 'a'" is shown in 4 examples, /u/ beside /ju/ in 3, the realization of /r/ in 3, the treatment of medial /t/ in 3, and the stressing of polysyllables in 2. All examples are in quasi-phonetic spelling.

279. Flaherty, N. "A World of 'Mixed-Up English.'" _Calgary Herald_, 12 Nov. 1963, p. 21 and 30.

This article records 24 expressions reported by a police officer in Calgary but does not limit their currency to CE alone.

280. Fong, William. "Canadian English Spelling." _English Language Teaching_, 22 (1968), 266-71.

This article describes CE spelling as a compromise between that of BE and that of AE. It cites 7 AE and 4 BE spellings that most Canadians would avoid and gives the Canadian versions of 11 features and 63 words in which British and American practices differ from each other. The usage of Canadian newspapers and textbooks is mentioned, and 11 examples are cited to show the confusion general in Canada.

281. French, William. "Eau Canada, Gloria's unfree." _Globe and Mail_ (Toronto), 15 Sept. 1973, p. 32.

This article reviews _Canajan, Eh?_ by Mark M. Orkin, q.v., and _CDC_, whose editors were led by Walter J. Avis. It gives detailed comments on 4 entries from Canajan, Eh? and refers to another 20; it also quotes Orkin's version of the first verse of O Canada. The relationship of CDC to DCHP is noted, and 16 of its entries are cited.

282. Friesen, John, "Ain't Ain't Hit Full Status Yet." Times-Journal (Fort William, Ont.), 1 Nov. 1963, p. 4.

This review welcomes ID for its recognition that CE exists and gives 14 examples to show ID as a valuable piece of Canadiana. It claims ID is too narrow in defining homebrew and in its usage label on ain't.

283. Fruman, Natalie. "Counter Culture." Maclean's Magazine, Mar. 1973, p. 34-35.

This article defines 6 words and phrases in use in the quick-lunch trade in Canada and gives the regional distribution of 4 of them.

284. Fulford, Robert. "Talk Canadian." SatN, May 1974, p. 9-10.

Drawing attention to an advertisement in Le Soleil seeking a teacher whose English has a Canadian accent, this article comments on the implication that someone exists who can recognize one.

285. Funk and Wagnalls Standard College Dictionary: Canadian Edition. Toronto: Fitzhenry and Whiteside, 1973.

The front matter in this dictionary includes a pronunciation key, specimen entries explained in detail, an essay on the history of the English language, and the essay "Canadian English" by Walter S. Avis, q.v. It also gives a section on the plan of the dictionary, with detail on pronunciations, level and style labels, etymologies, and synonyms. There is a table of English spellings. The dictionary contains over 150,000 entries and includes many Canadianisms.

286. Galinsky, Hans. Die Sprache des Amerikaners. 2 vols. Berlin: Langenscheidt, 1951 and 1952.

Vol. 1 mentions Canadian nasalization (p. 34) but gives no detail about it. It also speculates (p. 159-60) on the role of the Loyalists in forming CE. Vol. 2 notes (p. 149-51) that the construction happen + (pro)noun object appears in Nova Scotia, but the author ascribes it to pre-Loyalist English rather than to Scottish origins.

287. Ganong, W.F. "Algonkian Words in American English." JAF, 16 (1903), 128.

This reports the author's observation that bogan (thought to be from Indian pokologan), Pabineau (through Acadian French from Indian pimbina), and pung are in use in New Brunswick.

288. __________. "The Identity of the Animals and Plants Mentioned by the Early Voyagers to Eastern Canada and Newfoundland." PTRSC, 3rd Series, Vol. 3 (1909), Sec. II, p. 197-242.

This article gives evidence for the early use of 39 words later recorded in DCHP. It also gives an extended note on each word, classifying 5 as of unknown origin, 4 as extensions of European meanings, 19 as transfers thereof, 8 as borrowings, and 3 as inventions.

289. Geikie, Rev. A. Constable. "Canadian English." Canadian Journal of Science, Literature and History, 2 (1857), 344-55. Reprinted in "Readings on Language in Canada." Ed. Ronald H. Southerland (q.v.). p. 4-18.

The author objects to the Canadian coining of new words and use of recognized words in improper ways, the criterion of propriety being the author's impression of British usage. He cites 41 lexical and 8 morphological examples. He ends with a plea that educated men, teachers, and writers should cling to the practices of Shakespeare, Bacon, Dryden, and Addison.

290. Goetsch, Paul. "Das kanadische Englisch." Anglia, 81 (1963), 56-81.

The author reviews the theories of the origin of CE and relates the phenomena of CE to the settlement pattern of Canada. He then surveys the qualities of CE. On intonation, no conclusion can as yet be reached. In its rhythm, CE is generally closer to AE than to BE. In phonology, he mentions 9 features, including the realization of /r/, the use of /æ/ where BE has /ɑ/, and the distinctive allophones of /aɪ/ and /aʊ/. Under vocabulary, the development of DCE is forecast, and 6 classes of Canadianisms are exemplified; the strength of American influence is assessed. A survey of field records ends by denying that CE is entirely uniform, even outside the Maritimes. Specimens of Newfoundland speech illustrate the dialectal variety of CE. The article is thoroughly documented throughout.

291. Gordon, Barbara, and Anita Stevens. "A Comparison of New Brunswick and Saskatchewan English." CWPL, 1:1 (1975), 8-16.

This article is based partly on the transcriptions in "Canadian English and its Relation to Eighteenth Century American Speech" by Morton W. Bloomfield, q.v., and partly on the authors' own work. It discusses the presence of long vowels in New Brunswick and their absence from Saskatchewan (11 examples), and the voicing of intervocalic "t" [sic] in Saskatchewan but not in New Brunswick (3 examples). The variation between initial [h] and [hw], the variation in "Canadian Raising," and the devoicing of final fricatives are also discussed, with 9, 32, and 6 examples respectively.

292. Gove, Philip B. "Englishes of Other Lands." QJS, 52 (1966), 125-30.

This article claims that the number of Canadianisms in CE is astonishingly small. What few there are seem to come from the classified advertisements or the society pages of the newspapers.

293. Gowan, Derwin. Review of Canajan, Eh? by Mark M. Orkin. Brunswickan (Univ. of New Brunswick student newspaper), 5 Oct. 1973, p. 20.

This review compliments Orkin for "wittily and brilliantly" illustrating some of Canada's institutions and quotes 9 of Orkin's entries. It includes a brief biography of Orkin.

294. [Grace, John W.] "From Abatteau to Zombie: A Dictionary of Canadianisms." Ottawa Journal, 9 Dec. 1967, p. 6. Reprinted as "Canadianism Meaning," and as "Canadianisms Catalogued," both Anon. (q.v.)

This review of DCHP first cites its definition of a Canadianism and then mentions its use as an indication of Canadian linguistic fertility, exemplifying this by quoting an entry.

DCHP's quotations are exemplified and its dating for 3 entries is questioned. Its value as a repository of Canadian identity is shown by the noticing of 30 of its words referring to various aspects of Canadian life.

295. Grah, Ed. "Progress to Nationhood Highlighted in Dictionary." *Albertan* (Calgary), 19 Nov. 1960, p. 12.

This report of a talk by M.H. Scargill points out that DCE, then in preparation, will mirror Canadian culture and give usage-based criteria for CE. It explains why CE is ignored or distorted in British and American dictionaries and cites 29 Canadianisms so treated. It also comments that DCE will remove the instability of Canadian spelling.

296. Graham, Jean. "The Canadian Voice." *Canadian Magazine of Politics, Science, Art and Literature*, 26 (Nov. 1905-Apr. 1906), 483-84.

This article alleges that Canadian women of Halifax and Vancouver sound more like British women than women from the provinces between do. It also mentions that Canadians often ridicule those who speak with a British accent and notes the Canadian preference for a front vowel in *palm*, etc.

297. __________. "The Spring Colonists." *Canadian Magazine of Politics, Science, Art and Literature*, 27 (May-Oct 1906), 80-81.

This article advises the immigrant to avoid using *gum* for "mucilage " but recommends "of course" instead of *sure* and "shop" and "tram" instead of their American counterparts.

298. Graham, Robert Somerville. "The Anglicization of German Family Names in Western Canada." *AS*, 30 (1955), 260-64.

This article exemplifies 32 phonological changes made in anglicizing German names in Progress, Gross Lake, Hart's Hill, and Luseland, all in western Saskatchewan. Some German names remain almost unchanged, despite the existence of closely similar English names. Where an anglicized and a German form of a name exist, social conditions are likely to cause the anglicized form to survive.

Graham, Robert Somerville. Cont'd.

299. __________. "The Transition from German to English in the German Settlements of Saskatchewan." *JCLA*, 3 (1957), 9-13.

This article compares the usages of younger and older (born pre-1925) speakers in Luseland, Sask. It exemplifies their contrasting treatments of 19 phonemes and of English stress. German influence is shown in 3 syntactical and 6 lexical items, and 5 German phrases are noted. The disappearance of German from the area is forecast.

300. Gray, Malcolm. "I had a few clothings mostly they were hand-me-downs." *Globe and Mail* (Toronto), 24 Jan. 1975, p. 1.

This article includes a paragraph containing 1 morphological, 3 syntactical, and 2 spelling variants, and 1 variant idiom, to exemplify the English acceptable to some students at the University of British Columbia.

301. Greenleaf, Elizabeth B. "Newfoundland Words." *AS*, 6 (1930-1931), 306.

This is a brief plea for the collection of Newfoundland words as being either survivals from Elizabethan or "picturesque" coinages. The article gives 3 examples.

302. Gregg, R.J. "The diphthongs əi and aɩ in Scottish, Scotch-Irish and Canadian English." *CJL*, 18 (1973), 136-45.

This article exemplifies the need for a multidimensional concept of evidence, if proper explanations are to be given of diachronic and synchronic phonological phenomena. It considers MnE [əi] and [aɩ] as reflexes of ME /ī/ and, in the light of evidence from Scottish and Scotch-Irish, sees the second as the lowering of the first. The Canadian distribution of the diphthongs is seen as a generalization of a rule already in the grammar of English as a multidimensional language. The relevant phonological history is then presented in four rules, each representing a different stage of progression, and each evidenced by examples from different dialects.

Gregg, R.J. Cont'd.

303. _________. "The Linguistic Survey of British Columbia: The Kootenay Region," in Canadian Languages in Their Social Context. Ed. Regna Darnell. Edmonton: Linguistic Research, 1973, p. 105-16.

This article is based on a postal survey of 9 adults and 2 teenagers and on face-to-face interviews with 15 adults and 81 teenagers, all made with a questionnaire of 172 items. Within the Kootenays, 11 phonological items, 8 pairs of riming words, and 10 lexical items show that the teenagers tend to polarize on only one of the adults' options. The author cautiously hypothesizes a tendency, strengthening as one goes east, to polarize on the form current in the nearest AE.

304. _________. "Neutralisation and Fusion of Vocalic Phonemes in Canadian English as Spoken in the Vancouver Area." JCLA, 3 (1957), 78-83.

In this article, the author classes into 11 phonemes the vowels described in his "Notes on the Pronunciation of Canadian English as Spoken in Vancouver, B.C.," q.v. However, before intervocalic /r/, the author finds that as few as 5, and never more than 7, contrastive vowels occur. The author suggests that, when two phonemes are thus replaced by a phone intermediate between their allophones, the term "neutralisation" be used. He further suggests that, when only one phoneme is found in place of the expected two or more, this be described by the term "fusion," binary or tertiary. Special symbols are suggested for the phonemes resulting from neutralization and fusion.

305. _________. "Notes on the Pronunciation of Canadian English as Spoken in Vancouver, B.C." JCLA, 3 (1957), 20-26.

This article is based on data from approximately 50 Vancouver informants aged from 16 to 22. It identifies 20 vocalics (130 examples) and 24 consonantals in their speech. The article notes the loss of chronemic distinctions and the development of centering diphthongs in place of the former short vowels. Notes are added on 7 consonantals, alone or in sequences.

306. _________. "The Phonology of Canadian English as Spoken in the Area of Vancouver, British Columbia," in "Readings on Language in Canada." Ed. Ronald H. Southerland (q.v.). p. 34-54. Reprinted in Canadian

<u>English: Origins and Structures</u>. Ed. J.K. Chambers (q.v.). p. 133-44.

This is a reprint of "Neutralisation and Fusion of Vocalic Phonemes in Canadian English as Spoken in the Vancouver Area" and of "Notes on the Pronunciation of Canadian English as Spoken in Vancouver, B.C.," both by R.J. Gregg, q.v. A note is added, classifying the diphthongs under /aɪ/, /aʊ/, and /ɔɪ/.

307. Greig, J.Y.T. <u>Breaking Priscian's Head</u>. London: Kegan Paul, Trench, Trubner, [1929].

The author comments on the possibility that CE will progressively approximate AE (p. 9) and on the opposite possibility that the dialectal differentiation of English may be arrested by agreement (p. 11). He comments also on the Canadian use of American idioms (p. 13) and theorizes as to whether CE is actually becoming daily closer to AE (p. 30).

308. Gullon, Patricia. "A Comparison of M. Bloomfield's 'Western (Saskatchewan)' Dialect and a Dialect from the Regina Area." <u>CWPL</u>, 1:1 (1975), 17-21.

This article compares the dialect transcribed in "Canadian English and its Relation to Eighteenth Century American Speech" by Morton W. Bloomfield, q.v., to 5 Regina area dialects known to the author. The author denies Bloomfield's contention that all unstressed vowels become [ə] and questions the accuracy of Bloomfield's statement on the distribution of [a], [ɔ], and [ɒ]. Phonetic transcriptions of 44 words spoken by the 5 Regina speakers form the Appendix.

309. Gurr, Jon. "Cardboard Hero." <u>Weekend Magazine</u>, 1 Nov. 1975, p. 22 and 24-25.

This article includes a glossary of 15 words used by Canadian children in playing certain card games. The body of the article defines 6 more such words.

310. H., P.L. "Coming of Age Etymologically in First Canadian Dictionary." <u>Albertan</u> (Calgary), 18 Mar. 1967

This review of <u>SD</u> assesses it from a user's viewpoint and finds it satisfactory. A classification of the content of each entry in <u>SD</u> is given, and <u>SD</u>'s position in DCE is noted.

311. Hale, Edward E. "Geographical Terms in the Far West." DN, 6 (1932), 217-34.

This glossary reports the occurrence of barrens, bench 'land above a plain,' brush, bush, canyon, and coulee from western Canada.

312. Halkett, Andrew. Check List of the Fishes of the Dominion of Canada and Newfoundland. Ottawa: King's Printer, 1913.

This check list includes an index giving 886 vernacular names for fishes in Canada. Each name is cross-referenced to its scientific equivalent.

313. Hamilton, Donald E. "The English Spoken in Montreal: A Pilot Study." M.A. thesis. Univ. de Montréal, 1958.

The main part of this thesis, the analysis of findings, is reported at length in "Notes on Montreal English" by Donald E. Hamilton, q.v.

314. ________. "Notes on Montreal English." JCLA, 4 (1958), 70-79. Reprinted in Canadian English: Origins and Structures. Ed. J.K. Chambers (q.v.). p. 46-54.

After describing his investigation, the author reports that Montrealers preferred the American over the British term in 28 of 40 lexical items and the British in 12. In 3 phonological features, they preferred the American and, in 2, the British practice. Of individual words, 7 were given British and 6 American pronunciations. The American maintenance of secondary stress in polysyllables occurs among Montrealers, but their use of /i/ and /o/ in unstressed positions may be a Canadianism. Of 3 syntactic items, 2 show Americanism, while, of 2 idioms, 1 is American and 1 possibly French in origin. There are many comparisons with Ontario speech, as described in the articles "Speech Differences Along the Ontario-United States Border, etc.," by Walter S. Avis, q.v.

315. ________. "Standard Canadian English: Pronunciation," in Proceedings of the Ninth International Congress of Linguists. Ed. Horace G. Lunt. The Hague: Mouton, 1964. p. 456-59.

Based on the responses to 230 mailed questionnaires, this study concludes that there is a standard Canadian pronunciation and that it is becoming Americanized. The American influence is

Hamilton, Donald E. Cont'd.

demonstrated in 4 features of speech (19 examples) and in 7 individual words. British practice appears in 2 features (9 examples) and 3 words. Explanations are offered for this progressive Americanizing, whose continuation is forecast.

316. ________. "Standard Canadian English: Pronunciation." Summarized in Preprints of Papers for the Ninth International Congress of Linguists. Ed. M. Halle. Cambridge, Mass.: n.p., 1962. p. 38-39.

This is a summary, in about 350 words, of item 315 hereof.

317. Hamilton, Robert M., comp. Canadian Quotations and Phrases: Literary and Historical. Toronto: McClelland and Stewart, 1952. Reprinted, Canadian Bestseller Library. Toronto: McClelland and Stewart, 1965.

There are quotations relevant to CE on p. 23, 29, 116, and 152 of this work.

318. Hanley, Lloyd G. "Functions of Argot among Heroin Addicts," in Canada: A Sociological Profile. Comp. W.E. Mann. Toronto: Copp, Clark, 1968. p. 480-88.

The data in this article are based on tape-recorded interviews with 27 Toronto drug addicts. The functions of argot are discussed, and the author gives 24 examples of argot words or phrases and 4 one-paragraph statements in argot, translating where the need arises.

319. Harrington, Lyn. "Chinook Jargon." Beaver, No. 289 (Winter 1958), p. 26-29.

This records 12 Chinook Jargon words which have passed into CE.

320. Harris, Barbara Pritchard. "Selected Political, Cultural and Socio-Economic Areas of Canadian History as Contributors to the Vocabulary of Canadian English." Ph.D thesis. Univ. of Victoria, Victoria, B.C., 1975. See DAI A, 37 (1976), 3589A.

Basing her research on DCHP, the author sets out to show how

Harris, Barbara Pritchard. Cont'd.

Canadian history has affected and is reflected by CE, to show that periods of economic, social, or political activity have been followed by periods of linguistic activity, and to examine which linguistic means have been most productive lexically. The first two objects of the study are achieved. The third shows compounding as the most important lexical device in CE, the next being borrowing. (The foregoing was prepared from the summary in DAI A.)

321. _________, and Joseph F. Kess. "Salmon Fishing Terms in British Columbia." Names, 23 (1975), 61-66.

This article claims that the existence of differences in salmon-fishing terminology among the various forms of CE and AE "can be underscored by the unique ethnolinguistic paradigm exhibited by British Columbians in respect to . . . salmon fishing." It then gives and defines 20 names for the 5 species of Pacific salmon and gives derivations for 5 of them. It defines 8 names for stages of growth, 4 being etymologized and 3 noted as having special meanings in British Columbia. It explains 3 names for methods of fishing and 14 for equipment.

322. Harris, Sydney J. "Advice for Some Microphone Jockeys." Telegraph-Journal (Saint John, N.B.), 26 Mar. 1973, p. 4.

This article uses quasi-phonetic spelling to describe and correct 27 mispronunciations stated as common among broadcasters, presumably in Canada.

323. _________. "Strictly Personal." Mail-Star (Halifax N.S.), 10 Sept. 1973, p. 6.

Included in this collection of oddities in the BE pronunciation of personal names, etc., are records of 6 usages in which CE differs from BE.

324. Hébert, Maurice. "La pureté de la langue française et de la langue anglaise au Canada." PTRSC, 3rd Series, Vol. 32 (1938), Sec. I, p. 149-63.

This article mentions slang, U.S. influence, and dialectalisms as current in CE. It takes as standard the criterion of correctness of The Waverley Pictorial Dictionary and claims Sir Wilfrid Laurier as the public speaker who, in Canada, has made the most ringing use of the full resources of the CE verb.

325. Helliwell, M. MacLean. "Womans [sic] Sphere." Canadian Magazine of Politics, Science, Art and Literature, 19 (May-Oct. 1902), 555-56.

On the basis of her own observation, the author complains of the "slip-shod pronunciation, very unpleasant intonation and lamentably unmodulated voice of the average speaker" of CE. She ends with a plea for voice training.

326. Hempl, George. "Grease and Greasy." DN, 1 (1896), 438-44. Reprinted in Readings in American Dialectology. Ed. Harold B. Allen and Gary N. Underwood (q.v.). p. 154-59.

This article notes that 80% or more of those Canadians in Ontario, Quebec, and New Brunswick whose speech was surveyed by the author preferred /s/ in both grease and greasy.

327. Hench, Atcheson L. "Snow Shovel—a Canadianism." AS, 39 (1964), 299-300.

This article cites evidence to show that snow shovel is not a Canadianism, although it is so described in "Is There a Distinctive Literary Canadian English?" by Christopher Dean, q.v.

328. Hermite, Elisabeth. Review of A Dictionary of Canadianisms on Historical Principles, Walter S. Avis, Ed.-in-Chief. Bulletin des bibliotheques de France, 14th year, No. 2, Feb. 1969. p. 134.

This review outlines the history of DCHP and mentions its objective and its criterion of Canadianism. It draws attention to the many borrowings in CE, specifying some of their origins and exemplifying their interest. The pattern of each entry in DCHP is also described.

329. Hewson, John. "Larch, Tamarack and Juniper." RLS, No. 4 (1 May 1972), p. 1-4.

This article objects to DCHP's derivation of hackmatack and tamarack from Algonkian (Abenaki akemantak 'wood for snow shoes') as (1) the larch was not used for snow shoes and (2) the Algonkian name for the larch is unlike either hackmatack or tamarack. It also points out that in Newfoundland the larch is called the "juniper."

330. Hicks, Wessely. "Talk With A Twist." Toronto Telegram, 13 Mar. 1958, p. 7.

This article gives 45 expressions stated to be used by inmates of penitentiaries but, although written in a town containing a penitentiary, does not relate the expressions to any specific institution.

331. Higinbotham, John D. "Western Vernacular." Alberta Historical Review, 10 (1962), 9-17.

Based on the author's personal observation in southern Alberta, this article cites 276 westernisms, ranging from single words to complete sentences. It also cites 49 western personal nicknames and 23 "peculiar" western place-names. Quasi-phonetic spelling is used to record 26 phonological features and 3 morphological and 7 syntactical items.

332. Hillinger, Charles. "Islands Thrive on Kraut and Haddock." Los Angeles Times, 3 Aug. 1975, Pt. vi, p. 2-3.

This article records 5 phonological, 3 syntactical, and 2 lexical items from the speech of the Tancook Islands in Nova Scotia. The phonological items are in quasi-phonetic spelling.

333. ________. "Sauerkraut and salt fish keep islanders happy." Montreal Star, 6 Aug. 1975, p. B-2.

This is an abbreviated reprint of "Islands Thrive on Kraut and Haddock" by the same author, q.v.

334. Hogg, Hon. F.D. "Words and Terms for Court Proceedings." Globe and Mail (Toronto), 7 Dec. 1957, p. 6.

The author objects to 3 words and a form of address which he regards as misapplied when used of Canadian courts of justice.

335. House, A.B. "Spacewarp." Globe Magazine (Toronto), 25 Dec. 1970, p. 18.

This article records 10 features of Maritime speech observed by the author in Fredericton, N.B.

336. Howey, Mel. "Canadian Words Need Dictionary." London Free Press, 5 Feb. 1957, p. 1.

This report of a talk by Walter S. Avis cites 12 words whose variations of pronunciation, spelling, or meaning show the need for the DCE. The then state of the DCE project is summarized, and its function is stated to be descriptive, not legislatory.

337. ________. "Professor Notes Need of Canadian Dictionary." London Evening Free Press, 5 Feb. 1957, p. 31.

This is an abbreviated reprint of "Canadian Words Need Dictionary" by Mel Howey, q.v.

338. Hultin, Neil C. "Canadian Views of American English." AS, 42 (1967), 243-60.

The author notes that from time to time Canadians have held that AE was poorer than CE and was corrupting it. The presence of Americanisms in CE is remarked on, as are the avoidance of /ɑ/ in "palm, calm, bath, etc.," and the preservation of /j/ in news, avenue, and duty.

339. Hunter, Alfred C. Glossary of unfamiliar and other interesting words in The Newfoundland Journal of Aaron Thomas. St. John's, Nfld.: Memorial Univ. of Newfoundland, 1970.

After a brief introduction on the glossarist's method, this glossary defines 188 words from its source. At least one quotation from the source is given for each word, and a brief note on each adduces other relevant information.

340. Hutchison, Bill. "Verbal vandals throwing stones." Whig-Standard (Kingston), 24 Feb. 1975, p. 37.

This article records 11 lexical items of scientific origin now in the common vocabulary, presumably in Canada.

341. James, Geoffrey. "Canadian English: It's a Little Different, Eh?" Time, Canada Ed., 4 Jan, 1971, p. 11.

This review of Speaking Canadian English by Mark M. Orkin,

q.v., summarizes what Orkin says of the history of CE and of Canadian practice in spelling, vocabulary, pronunciation, lexical coinages, and parliamentary invective. It ends by outlining Orkin's forecast of the future of CE.

342. Jennings, Cecil. "Canada considers a U-turn into non-U." Globe and Mail (Toronto), 22 May 1975, p. 10.

This article reports some of the views that the reviser of the Canadian Government Style Manual for Writers and Editors holds on the terminal spelling -our, on hyphenation, and on the punctuation of acronyms.

343. ________. "To John A., it was a matter of honour" Globe and Mail (Toronto), 29 May 1975, p. 3.

This article records how the spelling -our in words such as honour was made official in Canada by an order-in-council dated 12 June 1890 , issued probably in deference to the opinion of the then Prime Minister, Sir John A. Macdonald, that this was "the mode now accepted by the best authorities now in England."

344. Johnston, C.M. Review of A Dictionary of Canadianisms on Historical Principles, Walter S. Avis, Ed.-in-Chief. Commentator (Toronto), 12:3 (Mar. 1968), 29.

This review outlines the history of DCHP and comments on the many Canadianisms it contains. It also comments on their etymologies and cites 4 of them. The documentation of DCHP's entries is mentioned, as is the effectiveness of its quotations, of which 4 are cited.

345. Jones, Brenda. "Rule Ordering in Canadian English." CWPL, 1:1 (1975), 29-34.

This paper discusses rule ordering in an Ontario dialect and in another, unidentified dialect. A rule for the voicing of [t] is deduced from 40 examples, and a rule for vowel shortening from 14. The results of differences in ordering these rules are examined in 49 examples, and it is noted that one pattern of ordering has supervened.

346. Jones, J.E.A. Review of *A Dictionary of Canadianisms on Historical Principles*, Walter S. Avis, Ed.-in-Chief. *Educational Courier* (Published by the Federation of Women Teachers' Associations of Ontario and the Ontario Public School Men Teachers' Federation), 40:3 (Dec. 1969-Jan. 1970), 7.

This review of *DCHP* quotes its purpose of providing "a historical record of words . . . characteristic of . . . Canadian life " and of providing the meanings of these. Exemplifying *DCHP*'s success in achieving this, the review quotes 2 of its entries and notes *DCHP*'s function in preserving Canada.

347. Joos, Martin. "A Phonological Dilemma in Canadian English." *Language* 18 (1942), 141-44. Reprinted in *Canadian English: Origins and Structures*. Ed. J.K. Chambers (q.v.). p. 79-82.

The author's summary of this article states: "The Canadian diphthongs /aj, aw/ have higher initial tongue-position in pre-fortis context than elsewhere, while for all other syllabics there is only a difference in length in the two kinds of context. This situation seems to fulfill a criterion of possible phonemicizing of the phonetic varieties of /aj, aw/. Moreover, the voicing of ambisyllabic /t/ makes it possible for the phonetic varieties to contrast before /d/. Contrast in other contexts may follow by analogy. Thus the possibility that /aj, aw/ may become four phonemes instead of two is demonstrable, but of course the probability is not."

348. Jordan, John. "Induction to Dialect." *Newfoundland Quarterly*, 65:3 (1967), 23-26.

This article gives Irish Gaelic etymologies for 50 words or morphemes from the lists of Newfoundlandisms in *Historic Newfoundland* by L.E.F. English, q.v., and in "Newfoundland Folk and Word Lore," in *Folklore of Newfoundland in Old Words, Phrases, and Expressions* by P.K. Devine, q.v.

349. K., I. "Dictionaries." *Voxair* (Canadian Forces Base, Winnipeg), 27 Mar. 1968, p. 6.

This notes the adoption of *SD* as the standard reference work for the *Toronto Telegram* and adds a brief statistical account of the works constituting DCE, together with a biographical note on Walter S. Avis.

350. Kasatkina, T.I. "O nekotoryx tendencijax upotreblenija soslagatel'nogo naklonenija I v anglijskom jazyke Kanady: Na materiale poèzii 19-20vv.," in Voprosy Lingvistiki, Vypusk 116. Ed. G.P. Boguslavskaja. Jaroslavl: Jaroslavskij ordena T.K.Z. gos. pedagog. inst. im. K.D. Ušinskogo, 1974.

The authors were unable to obtain a copy of this work in time to annotate it. The 1975 MLA International Bibliography: Volume III, Linguistics notes (p. 111, item 6400) "Subjunctive in Canadian Eng.: Examples from poetry."

351. Kemp, Leanne. "The Glottal Closure Sound in English." CWPL, 1:1 (1975), 35-36.

A tentative rule, based on 36 examples, is formed to explain the pattern of the occurrence of glottalization of /t/ in Albertan speech.

352. Kenyon, John Samuel, and Thomas Albert Knott. A Pronouncing Dictionary of American English. Springfield Mass.: G. and C. Merriam, 1944. Reprinted 1953.

The preface notes that the dictionary contains "occasional references" to Canadian pronunciation and instances the Canadian pronunciation of dahlia. The front matter notes the Canadian use of [a], the CE instability of [ɔ] except pre-/r/, as also the Canadian use of [ɛ] for [æ] before /r/, and it gives 4 examples of this, together with 2 examples of the high onset of Canadian /aʊ/ and /aɪ/. It also gives 9 words whose pronunciation in CE resembles their pronunciation in BE.

353. Kerner, Fred. "A Word to the Wise." CAB, 49:1 (Fall 1973), 18.

This article comments disapprovingly on tautology in CE, giving 1 example thereof.

354. ________. "A Word to the Wise." CAB, 49:3 (Spring 1974), 23.

This article comments disapprovingly on the phrase try and, said to be gaining currency in CE.

Kerner, Fred. Cont'd.

355. __________. "A Word to the Wise." *CAB*, 49:4 (Summer 1974), 20.

This article comments disapprovingly on the expressions *for free* and *saw*, *break*, etc., *in half*.

356. __________. "A Word to the Wise." *CAB*, 50:1 (Fall 1974), 21.

This article comments disapprovingly on the television broadcasters' ignoring of the difference in meaning of *majority* and *plurality*, on their use of *ethnic*, and on their use of *standings* to mean 'relationship.'

357. __________. "A Word to the Wise." *CAB*, 50:2 (Winter 1974), 18.

This article comments disapprovingly on the use by Canadian writers of the expressions *the hoi polloi*, *rice paddy*, *the La Scala*, *Mt. Fujiyama*, the *Sahara Desert*, *criminally insane*, and *new record*, and on their treatment of *fulsome* and *replica*.

358. __________. "A Word to the Wise." *CAB*, 50:4 (Summer 1975), 18.

This article comments disapprovingly on the use of *hopefully* for 'it is hoped,' of *presently* for 'at present,' and of *momentarily* for 'soon.' It also deprecates the redundant use of *personally*.

359. Kerr, Joy Wendie. "We Speak Canadian." *Mirror* (Scarborough-Don Mills, Ont.), 29 June 1966, p. 4A.

This pre-publication article on *DCHP* notes the distinctiveness of CE, and reports some statistics and other material provided by P.D. Drysdale. Dictionaries record history, new words developing as experience is described. The article refers to 6 word-producing phenomena and instances 13 new words. The continuation of Canadian linguistic inventiveness is shown by 9 Canadianisms. The article gives some details of the mechanics of dictionary production.

360. Keys, D.R. "Some Thoughts on English Pronunciation." Univ. of Toronto Monthly, No. 35 (Mar. 1935), p. 145.

The author claims that there is an increasing Americanization of CE, evidenced by the stressing of the first syllable of address, adult, inquiry, etc. Classical influence is said to account for a change in the stress and pronunciation of disciplinary and marital.

361. King, Robert D. Historical Linguistics and Generative Grammar. Englewood Cliffs, N.J.: Prentice-Hall, 1969.

Noting (p. 91) that some speakers of CE centralize /aɪ/ and /aʊ/ only before voiceless obstruents, the author goes on to say that other speakers of CE have generalized the centralizing rule to produce centralization of these diphthongs in all environments.

362. Kinloch, A.M. "The Study of Canadian English." English Teacher. Newsletter of the New Brunswick Teachers' Association Council of Teachers of English. 4:2 (Feb. 1975), 4-7. Reprinted, in part, in Canadian Council of Teachers of English Newsletter, 8:4 (May 1975), n. pag.

This article first exemplifies, in 3 phonological and 5 lexical features, the differences between BE and CE and then comments on the cultural adequacy of CE. The increasing public recognition of CE is noted, as is the increasing amount of scholarship, especially lexicographical, devoted to CE. The dialectal variety of CE is exemplified in 6 phonological items and 1 lexical item. The problems this variety poses for the teacher are mentioned and some solutions are suggested.

363. ________. "The Survey of Canadian English: A First Look at New Brunswick Results." EngQ, 5:4 (1972-1973), 41-51.

The author notes 29 phonological, 3 morphological, 2 syntactical, 2 idiomatic and lexical items, and 1 spelling item as formerly and possibly still dominant in New Brunswick. He shows 3 idiomatic and lexical items to be increasing in popularity. He sees 5 phonological, 1 syntactical, and 2 idiomatic and lexical items as common among the students, while 3 phonological, 1 morphological, and 8 lexical items evidence a generation gap. There is an attempt to assess the effectiveness of the SCE in New Brunswick.

Kinloch, A.M. Cont'd.

364. __________. "The Survey of Canadian English: Possible Evidence for Pronunciation." EngQ, 4:4 (Winter 1971), 59-65.

Based on written responses to 199 questionnaires distributed to 3 schools in New Brunswick, this article discusses the possibility of the existence of 1 syllabic feature, 11 phonological features, and 6 individual words in the province.

365. __________. "What's Happening in Canadian English?" University Perspectives (Univ. of New Brunswick newspaper), 20 Jan. 1975, p. 4-5.

After pointing out that CE is part of the Canadian national identity, the author evidences the growing recognition of this fact. He then surveys work completed and in progress at the time of writing.

366. Kirwin, William J.[1] "Additions to Previous Bibliographies." RLS, No. 3 (15 Jan. 1971), p. 23.

This bibliography lists 4 published works and 1 unpublished work on Newfoundland dialects. There is a brief comment on 1 item. The 4 items containing glossaries are starred.

367. __________. "Bibliography of Writings on Newfoundland English." RLS, No. 1 (1 Oct. 1968), p. 4-7.

This bibliography lists 41 books and articles, 1 pamphlet, and 7 unpublished papers containing information on Newfoundland dialects. There are brief comments on 6 items. The 23 items containing glossaries are starred.

368. __________. "'Black English' in Newfoundland?" RLS, No. 4 (1 May 1972), p. 33.

Referring to an unpublished paper by Raven I. McDavid, Jr., the author notes McDavid's suggestion that many linguistic features reported in studies of Black English occur in the speech of Newfoundland as well.

[1] Some of this author's works bear only his initials.

Kirwin, William J. Cont'd.

369. ________. "A Collection of Popular Etymologies in Newfoundland Vocabulary." RLS, No. 3 (15 Jan. 1971), p. 16-18.

This article lists the popular etymologies of 9 Newfoundland words. Correct etymologies are suggested for 3 of them.

370. ________. "Either for Any in Newfoundland." RLS, No. 1 (1 Oct. 1968), p. 8-10.

Citing what evidence is available so far, the author speculates, though with caution, that the origins of this Newfoundland usage may lie in the English West Country.

371. ________. "Ingressive Speech Reported in Newfoundland 'Mummer-talk.'" RLS, No. 3 (15 Jan. 1971), p. 24.

This article notes from Christmas Mumming in Newfoundland, ed. H. Halpert and G.M. Story (Toronto: Univ. of Toronto for Memorial Univ. of Newfoundland, 1969) the common occurrence of ingressive speech in Newfoundland mumming, and suggests that "[a study] of ingressive speech in England and elsewhere . . . might help explain its prevalence in Newfoundland."

372. ________. "Labrador, St. John's and Newfoundland: Some Pronunciations." JCLA, 6 (1960), 115-16.

This article describes 3 different pronunciations of Labrador, 3 of St. John's, and 5 of Newfoundland, all current to various specified degrees in the speech of older speakers in the Avalon Peninsula in Newfoundland.

373. ________. "Lines, Coves, and Squares in Newfoundland Names." AS, 40 (1965), 163-70.

This study gives the socio-historical origins of the Newfoundland use in toponymy of line for a cross-country road, of square for a short street otherwise not distinctive, and of cove for a street running where a stream once ran.

374. ________. "Linguistic Research in Newfoundland." RLS, No. 3 (15 Jan. 1971), p. 13-15.

This lists 2 published works, 2 unpublished works, and 9 works

Kirwin, William J. Cont'd.

in preparation, all relevant to Newfoundland dialect. It also lists 1 work in preparation on Cape Breton dialect.

375. ________. "Linguistic Research in Newfoundland." RLS, No. 4 (1 May 1972), p. 31-33.

This article lists 1 published, 1 unpublished, and 1 incomplete work relevant to Newfoundland dialect.

376. ________. "Linguistic Research in Newfoundland." RLS, No. 5 (21 Jan. 1974), p. 30-33.

This article lists 4 published items, 7 reviews, and 5 projects relevant to Newfoundland dialect.

377. ________. "Linguistic Research Materials in the Folklore Archive at Memorial University." RLS, No. 1 (1 Oct. 1968), p. 11-13.

This article describes the forms of field collecting used to create the Folklore Archive, the work being done there with printed and manuscript materials, and the location and state of the archive itself.

378. ________. "Newfoundland Usage in the 'Survey of Canadian English.'" RLS, No. 5 (21 Jan. 1974), p. 9-14.

This article comments on the linguistic preferences of Newfoundland and on their relationship to the national usages, as both appeared in the SCE. The results of 5 spelling items, 16 grammatical items, 15 lexical items, and 12 phonological items are so discussed. Information is added from the author's own research.

379. ________. "The Present State of Language Studies in Newfoundland." RLS, No. 1 (1 Oct. 1968), p. 1-3.

This article describes in specific terms research then in progress at Memorial University of Newfoundland and outlines the methods used to compile and control the "Newfoundland Vocabulary." The directions of current research are also indicated in more general terms.

Kirwin, William J. Cont'd.

380. _________. "Selecting and Presenting the Lexicon [in the Dictionary of Newfoundland English]." *RLS*, No. 6 (2 May 1975), p. 5-9.

This article describes some factors which have been important in the selection of material for inclusion in the forthcoming dictionary of Newfoundland English. The principal features of each entry are discussed, and some indication is given of problems posed by the material to be included under each feature.

381. _________. "Vocabulary in Aaron Thomas's *Newfoundland Journal* [1794-95]." *RLS*, No. 3 (15 Jan. 1971), p. 25.

This review of *A Glossary of Unfamiliar and Other Interesting Words in the Newfoundland Journal of Aaron Thomas* by Alfred C. Hunter, q.v., cites 11 examples to show the glossary's range.

382. Klawitter, Ursula. "Zum Jubiläum: Mukluk und trockene Biene." *Bunte Illustrierte* (Munich and Frankfurt), No. 13 (22 Mar. 1967), p. 5.

This review of *DCHP* comments on how it shows the individuality of CE and cites 6 of *DCHP*'s entries to support this.

383. Klyn, Doyle. "Chimo's the Word." *Weekend Magazine*, 17 Jan. 1970, p. 26-27.

In a note on the popularity of the word *chimo*, the author observes that it is pronounced "cheemo."

384. _________. "We Flunked Johnny's Spelling Test." *Weekend Magazine*, 1 Apr. 1972, p. 26-27.

This article notes 9 spelling errors observed in public notices, etc., in Canada.

385. Knight, Margaret Bennett. "Scottish Gaelic, English, and French: Some Aspects of the Macaronic Tradition of the Codroy Valley, Newfoundland." *RLS*, No. 4 (1 May 1972), p. 25-30.

This article notes that, in the area studied, conversations in English were "peppered" with Gaelic words. One inhabitant had to use the Gaelic word for the technical term wool-winder, and English-speaking dancers would use a Gaelic expression to encourage the musician. The author gives four macaronic texts, 3 English-Gaelic and 1 English-French.

386. Kurath, Hans. A Word Geography of the Eastern United States. Ann Arbor, Mich.: Univ. of Michigan, 1966.

There are comments on the vocabulary of New Brunswick on p. 13, 16, 20, 21, 22, 24, 25, 51, 58, 59, 60, 67, 69, and 78. In general, they show it as allied, through the Loyalists, to the vocabulary of New York and New Jersey and also as sharing in the coastal rather than the inland lexicon of AE. (The New Brunswick communities concerned are listed in the Handbook of the Linguistic Geography of New England by Hans Kurath and others, q.v.)

387. __________, with the collaboration of Marcus L. Hansen, Julia Bloch, and Bernard Bloch. Handbook of the Linguistic Geography of New England. Providence, R.I.: Brown Univ., and Washington, D.C.: American Council of Learned Societies, 1939. 2nd ed. rev. Audrey R. Duckert and Raven I. McDavid, Jr. New York: AMS Press, 1973.

This work includes brief biographies of the informants, of whom 8 represented the New Brunswick communities of: St. Stephen, Bay Side (St. Croix parish), White Head (Kingston parish), Saint John, Elm Hill (Hampstead parish), Lower Southampton, Hartland, and Woodstock.

388. __________, Miles L. Hanley, Bernard Bloch, Guy S. Lowman, Jr., and Marcus L. Hansen, eds. The Linguistic Atlas of New England. 3 vols. Providence, R.I.: Brown Univ., 1939-1943. Reprinted New York: AMS Press, 1972.

Information about the speech of 8 New Brunswick communities appears in phonetic script on the maps herein: St. Stephen, on 691 maps; Bay Side, on 551 maps; White Head, on 706 maps; Saint John, on 697 maps; Elm Hill, on 385 maps; Lower Southampton, on 309 maps; Hartland, on 647 maps; and Woodstock, on 702 maps.

389. __________, and Raven I. McDavid, Jr. The Pronunciation of English in the Atlantic States. Ann Arbor, Mich.: Univ. of Michigan, 1961.

The text gives information on pronunciation in "Canada,"

(p. 166), Ontario, (p. 144, 149), and New Brunswick, (p. 107-08, 148, 152, 158, 166, and 178). The maps, *passim*, give information on the pronunciation of the vowels in 142 words, of the consonants in 2 words, of the syllabication of 1 word, and of the complete pronunciation of 1 word from Kingston, Ont. For Prescott, Ont., the figures are 118, 2, 1, and 1, respectively. For Welland, Ont., they are 120, 2, 1, and 1.

390. L., M.A. "Compilation of Canada's 'Language' Delightfully Surprising." *Albertan* (Calgary), 27 Jan. 1968, p. 4.

This review of *DCHP* describes CE as "a cross between American slang and the most conservative English grammar." It points to the large numbers of Canadianisms in existence, giving 20 examples of these, and comments on the richness of the information in *DCHP*'s entries.

391. Labov, William. "The Social Motivation of a Sound Change." *Word*, 19 (1963), 273-309.

The author remarks (p. 281, fn. 21) that centralized versions of /aɪ/ and /aʊ/ are "well known as a feature of Canadian English, where the effect of the voiceless-voiced consonant environment is quite regular."

392. Langenfelt, Gösta. "*She* and *Her* instead of *It* and *Its*." *Anglia*, 70 (1951), 90-101.

The author points out that the generalization of the morpheme *she* was common in Scotch dialect, and in the English of francophone Canadians. These ethnic groups made up a large proportion of the population of early nineteenth-century Canada and may have played a part in the spread of this idiom.

393. Lardner, John. "Language Here and There." *New Yorker*, 26 Sept. 1959, p. 171-74.

This article reports 2 broadcasts on CE over CBM Montreal. According to one broadcaster, regionalisms survive in CE, despite growing standardization; the statement of 7 such regionalisms is attributed to Jack Peach. Donald E. Hamilton's contrast of AE-influenced Montreal English with the BE-influended language of Toronto is supported by 10 examples. The writer speculates that CE and Canadian French, both influenced by American television, etc., may one day coalesce.

394. Larsen, Thorleif, and Francis C. Walker. _Pronunciation: A Practical Guide to Spoken English in Canada and the United States_. Toronto: O.U.P., 1930.

Addressed to the layman, this dictionary attempts to record accepted usage. In Chapter IV, the authors have "grouped [more than 1,600] troublesome words according to the sounds usually given to the vowels that cause difficulty." In Chapter V, which deals with consonants, over 8,000 words are grouped by letters, not by sounds.

395. Larson, Cheryl. "Canadian Spoken Here, New Dictionary Shows." _Herald_ (Calgary), 17 Apr. 1969, p. 53.

Arguing that speaking CE makes Canadians identifiable, the author cites some 23 words from _DCHP_.

396. Lear, Henry. "Hibbs Cove Names for the Fishes of Conception Bay, Newfoundland." _RLS_, No. 3 (15 Jan. 1971), p. 1-6.

This article includes the IPA transcription of the local names for 10 parts of a fish and for 34 kinds of fish.

397. Lehn, Walter. "Vowel Contrasts in a Saskatchewan English Dialect." _JCLA_, 5 (1959), 90-98. Reprinted in _Canadian English: Origins and Structures_. Ed. J.K. Chambers (q.v.). p. 109-16.

Basing this study on his own Herschel, Sask., idiolect, the author first briefly discusses his consonant phonemes. In vocalics, his idiolect has 8 "simple" nuclei (including /ɨ/ and /ə/) and 14 "complex" nuclei; not all contrast in all contexts. Before /r/, there are only 9 contrasting nuclei and, before juncture, 15. The overall number of contrastive nuclei is 15.

398. Lighthall, W. Douw. "Canadian English." _Week_ (Toronto), 16 Aug. 1889, p. 581-83.

After denying that CE is non-dialectal and British-like, the author outlines Canada's settlement pattern and comments on the various CE dialects. A "Bluenose" dialect is evidenced from Haliburton; 1 French-derived feature thereof is noted. "Acadian Scotch" is exemplified in 8 features observed by "a local clergyman." Lower Canada shows 9 legal terms which are French or French-influenced; from Montreal, 37 general terms of like origin are quoted. The Eastern Townships are said to be heavily Americanized. For "Chateauguay Scotch," 19 features, including 3 Americanisms, are cited. Ontario is generally Loyalist with enclaves of other dialects. American influence is shown by 23 generally current features, while 20 Canadianisms are also cited. Western Canada shows 4 Americanisms and 3 Canadianisms. Finally, the author forecasts the gradual disappearance of dialects and the Briticization of CE.

399. Lortie, Paul. "Study of an Irish-Canadian pronunciation: a phonetic study." M.A. thesis. Univ. de Montréal, 1948.

This thesis reports the pronunciation of a bilingual Montrealer of Irish parentage, who is both native of and resident in that city. There is a detailed phonetic description of all the informant's vowels, diphthongs, and consonants; each phonetype is exemplified, and the vowels are plotted on the IPA grid. The phonetypes are then phonemicized, and their distribution is described

400. Love, Tracey. "An examination of *Eh* as Question Particle." B.A. thesis. Univ. of Alberta, 1973.

According to its Abstract, "this thesis discusses the Canadian *eh* and its role as question particle. It is shown that the *eh* particle acts alone and in conjunction with other interrogative markers, e.g., rising intonation, question words, to indicate a question. C.L. Baker's claim that no language can simultaneously mark its yes-no questions with a sentence-final particle and move question words to sentence-initial position, is thus contradicted."

401. Lovell, C.J. "Lexicographic Challenges of Canadian English." *JCLA*, 1, No. 1, Regular Series (Mar. 1955), 2-5.

This article examines how 12 words common in CE are treated in *OED*, *DAE*, and *DA*. All the citations in these dictionaries for 10 of the words can be antedated from Canadian sources, and the author thinks it probable that the same applies to the other 2. A footnote adds 13 more examples of Canadian antedatings of citations in *DAE* and *DA*.

402. __________. "A Sampling of Materials for a Dictionary of Canadian English Based on Historical Principles." *JCLA*, 4 (1958), 7-33.

After a brief explanation of the purpose of the sample entries,

Lovell, C.J. Cont'd.

in which are noted 16 Canadianisms omitted from the main glossary, this article gives 44 dictionary entries made up from Canadian sources and illustrating the content and format of a historical dictionary of CE.

403. ________. "Whys and Hows of Collecting for the Dictionary of Canadian English, I: Scope and Source Material." JCLA, 1, No. 2, Regular Series (Oct. 1955), 3-8.

This article discusses the difficulties in the way of producing the then proposed DCE. The scope of the work and the related definition of the term Canadian English are then considered. The author gives 27 words and phrases common in CE but unreliably treated in or completely absent from current dictionaries. He then defines 15 classes of Canadianisms, at least 5 examples being given of each class. Finally, the author makes a fourfold categorization of possible sources of CE.

404. ________. "Whys and Hows of Collecting for the Dictionary of Canadian English, II: Excerption of Quotations." JCLA, 2, No. 1, Regular Series (Mar. 1956), 23-32.

In the course of giving a detailed description of lexicographical method, this article incidentally cites 54 words and phrases exemplifying CE.

405. M., G.H. "Copycat Canadians." Letter to the editor. Toronto Daily Star, 18 Mar. 1957, p. 6.

This article records 1 lexical, 1 idiomatic, and 10 pronunciational items in which Canadians are adopting American practice.

406. M., J.B. "Do We Speak American?" Winnipeg Free Press, 20 June 1936, p. 29.

This review of The American Language by H.L. Mencken (4th ed., 1936), q.v., approves Mencken's general thesis that AE is becoming the standard and gives 3 instances of the spread of American words into CE.

407. Macaree, David (on front cover as David Maccaree). "Between You and I, It's Me." British Columbia Library Quarterly, 34:1 (July 1970), 9-11.

This article notes the frequency of it's me, and the spread of phrases such as between you and I in (presumably) CE.

408. MacDade, John. "The Split Infinitive." Canadian Commentator. 4:1 (Jan. 1960), 18.

This article notes that in a year of listening to CBC announcers its author heard no split infinitives.

MacDade, John. See also Davidson, Rev. J.A.

409. Macdonald, Sir John A. Minute of Council. 30 May 1890.

According to the Memoirs of Sir John A. Macdonald by Sir Joseph Pope, q.v., this minute recorded the then Prime Minister's opinion that in the spelling of words such as labour, etc., the only mode to be followed was that of the best BE authorities.

410. MacKenzie, Jim. "How 'Educated Canadians' Spell, Speak and Define." St. Catharines Standard (St. Catharines, Ont.), 25 Mar. 1967, p. 32.

This review of SD refers to 20 of its entries to illustrate 7 etymologies, 2 pronunciations, 8 spelling variations, and 1 definition, and it uses 10 examples to show SD's range. The place of SD in the DCE is given, and its editorship described. The number of entries, their content, and the principles of entry selection are all mentioned. The editors are reported to hold that "educated Canadians set their own standards."

411. M[aclellan], W.E. "Topics of the Day." DR, 7 (1927), 395-97.

This article notes the spread in CE of Americanized pronunciations recorded in quasi-phonetic spelling as "thuh," "wur," "whurfore," and "thurfore."

412. MacNamara, Francis J. "Toronto Writer Equally Culpable." Letter to the editor. Evening Citizen (Ottawa), 3 Nov. 1938, p. 28.

The writer objects to 4 cited features in the idiolect of a review by H.W. Freeman in SatN. (See also "When Homer Nods" by P.F. Spratt, q.v.)

413. Macodrum, William Boyd. "The Dialect of the Cape Breton Kelt." Canadian Bookman, 8 (1926), 125.

This article takes issue with writers who put Lowland Scots speech, of which 9 examples are given, into the mouths of fictional Cape Bretoners. True Cape Breton dialect is exemplified in 7 items of pronunciation and 7 of lexicon or idiom. A further 9 idioms observed in Nova Scotia are attributed to New England influence.

414. MacPhail, Sir Andrew. "Our Canadian Speech." SatN, 29 June 1935, p. 1-2. Reprinted in Yearbook of the Arts in Canada 1936. Ed. Bertram Brooker. Toronto: Macmillan of Canada, 1936. p. 235-39.

This article compares CE to BE in terms of beauty of sound and precision of diction, much to the detriment of the former. It maintains that there is no standard CE, merely a variety of accents, all more or less unpleasant.

415. MacPherson, H.L. "Now It's English Canadian." Windsor Star, 5 Feb. 1962, p. 9.

This review of BD gives its place in the DCE series and outlines its origin in the unsatisfactoriness for Canadians of British and American dictionaries, giving 4 examples of this. BD's range of entries is exemplified, as is its employment of usage labels. The reviewer cites 8 examples of BD's spelling policy, 2 examples to show its etymological, and 2 to show its semantic suitability to Canada.

416. Marckwardt, Albert H. "Want with Ellipsis of Verbs of Motion." AS, 23 (1948), 3-9.

This article draws attention to the currency in New Brunswick of the expression I want off, and cites it as evidence that the expression was brought to the United States by the Scotch and Scotch-Irish.

417. Massey, B.W.A. "Canadian Fish-Names in OED and DAE." N&Q, 200 (1955), 453-55; 201 (1956), 41-44 and 125-30; 202 (1957), 79-83, 173-77, and 203-08.

See the comment on item 418 of this Bibliography.

418. ________. "OED and DAE: Some Comparisons." N&Q, 199 (1954), 127-29, 493-97, and 522-25.

Despite the variation in the titles and the inconsistency of the section numbering, items 417 and 418 of this Bibliography are all parts of one study. The study concludes that 39 names of freshwater fish originated in Canada, through invention, borrowing, calquing, or other linguistic processes. All are listed at the end of the last article in the series. In passing, the author takes issue with DAE for its "slighting" of British sources and of CE.

419. Mathews, Mitford M. The Beginnings of American English. Chicago: Univ. of Chicago, 1931.

This book quotes (p. 143) the introduction to the Dictionary of Americanisms (1848) by John Russell Bartlett, who cites 9 words of French origin in CE.

420. ________. Review of A Dictionary of Canadianisms on Historical Principles, Walter S. Avis, Ed.-in-Chief. JEngL, 3 (Mar. 1969), 89-91.

After summarizing the front matter and introduction of DCHP, this review outlines DCHP's history and cites its definition of a Canadianism. The illustrations and the documentation of its quotations are also mentioned. The relationship of the material in DCHP to that in DAE is discussed, and the complementariness of DA and DCHP is illustrated by summarizing the information that each gives for thunderbird.

421. M[aurer], D.W. "Slang." New Encyclopedia Britannica: Macropædia. 16. Chicago: Encyclopedia Britannica, 1974, p. 850-53.

This article notes that CE and AE have much common slang, but that CE has more BE, French, and Amerindian slang than AE has.

422. McAree, J.V. "The Indispensable Book." Globe and Mail (Toronto), 6 Oct. 1949, p. 6.

Mainly a review of Webster's Collegiate Dictionary, this article mentions the Canadian acceptance of AE spellings in -or, as opposed to BE spellings in -our.

423. ________. "Words: British, American." Globe and Mail (Toronto), 20 Oct. 1949, p. 6.

Arguing that Canadians are too ready to adopt American linguistic habits, this article quotes, in support of its thesis, 1 idiom, 2 lexical items, 14 spellings, 3 features of pronunciation supported by 6 examples, and 5 further individual pronunciations, all said to be borrowed from AE into CE.

424. McAtee, W.L. "Bird Names with Animal or Plant Components." AS, 30 (1955), 176-85.

This article lists 14 local bird names from Newfoundland and Labrador, 1 from Prince Edward Island, 11 from Nova Scotia, 7 from New Brunswick, 2 from Quebec, 9 from Ontario, 6 from Manitoba, 5 from Saskatchewan, 1 from Alberta, and 2 from British Columbia. All have the type of linguistic structure mentioned in the title of the article.

425. ________. "The Eskimo Curlew as 'Fute.'" AS, 31 (1956), 299-300.

This records the use in Manitoba of foolish godwit for the Hudsonian godwit.

426. ________. "Facetious Monickers for American Birds." AS, 31 (1956), 180-87.

This article records 14 facetious names, current in various specified provinces of Canada, for 13 species of wild birds; it records also a further 2 names whose currency is given simply as "general."

427. ________. "Folk Etymology in North American Bird Names." AS, 26 (1951), 90-95.

After defining folk etymology, this article gives 16

McAtee, W.L. Cont'd.

Canadian names (denoting 8 species of birds), which have been subject to folk etymology; the province where each name is used is also given. A further 10 names, each denoting 1 species of bird and each subject to the process, are described as being in "general currency."

428. ________. Folk Names of Canadian Birds. National Museum of Canada Bulletin No. 149, Biological Series No. 51. 2nd ed. Ottawa: Department of Northern Affairs and Natural Resources, 1959.

This book lists 319 species of birds found in Canada. Under each species are given the English, French, and Gaelic folk-names for the species, together with some comment on the geographical distribution of each name and, occasionally, some other remarks. An index gives a list of all species mentioned.

429. ________. "'Stint' as a Bird Name." AS, 31 (1956), 299.

This article records the use in British Columbia of the word snippet for a species of small shore bird.

430. McCulloch, Walter F. Woods Words: A Comprehensive Dictionary of Loggers Terms. Portland, Oreg.: Oregon Historical Society and Champoeg Press, 1958.

This dictionary contains an estimated 4,900 entries defining Pacific coast lumbering terms. Its sources imply that some are in use in Canada, but none are so marked.

McDade, John. See Davidson, Rev. J.A.

431, McDavid, Raven I., Jr. "Canadian English." AS, 46 (1971), 287-89.

This review of Speaking Canadian English by Mark M. Orkin, q.v., points out that many articles which should have been used in preparing an overall treatment of CE do not appear in the bibliography of Orkin's work. It also criticizes Orkin's attitude to DCHP, his definition of Standard English, his use of the term General American, and his comment on the /r/-less dialects of AE.

McDavid, Raven I., Jr. Cont'd.

432. __________. "Dialects: British and American Standard and Nonstandard," in Linguistics Today. Ed. Archibald A. Hill. New York: Basic Books, 1969. p. 79-88.

This essay notes that local varieties of English are strongest in the areas of early settlement, e.g., the Atlantic Provinces. It contrasts the prestige of BE with the growing linguistic autonomy of Canada. It remarks on and exemplifies 2 general likenesses between CE and Inland Northern AE and comments on 3 differences between them.

433. __________. "The Dialects of American English," in The Structure of American English by W. Nelson Francis. New York: Ronald, 1958. Ch. 9.

This account surveys passim the then state of scholarship on CE and, mainly from the articles "Speech Differences Along the Ontario-United States Border [I, etc.]" by Walter S. Avis, q.v., it gives 3 phonological and 8 lexical features and 1 idiom from CE.

434. __________. "The Folk Vocabulary of New York State." NYFQ, 7 (1951), 173-92.

Although almost entirely concerned with AE, this article notes that coal oil, dew worm, shivaree, and stook have penetrated southwards from the Canadian border.

435. __________. "Linguistic Geography in Canada: An Introduction." JCLA, 1, No. 1 (Oct. 1954), 3-8.

After citing 1 phonological and 1 syntactical example of CE as a dialect, this article outlines the history and development of the LAUSC project in the United States and Canada. It gives special attention to the principles of informant selection and to method in general.

436. __________. "Midland and Canadian Words in Upstate New York." AS, 26 (1951), 248-56.

Based on data from the LAUSC records, this study reports 4 Canadian terms, shivaree, stook, dew worm, and coal oil as being common in upstate New York. On the other hand, political terms, such as county town, had not crossed the political boundary.

McDavid, Raven I., Jr. Cont'd.

437. __________. "The Principal Dialect Areas of the United States," in _Contemporary English: Change and Variation_. Ed. David L. Shores (q.v.). p. 26-41.

This is a reprint of the concluding paragraphs, which include the Canadian material, of "The Dialects of American English" by the same author, q.v.

438. __________. Review of _A Dictionary of Canadianisms on Historical Principles_, Walter S. Avis, Ed.-in-Chief. _CJL_, 13 (1967), 55-57.

This review of _DCHP_ mentions the firmness of the execution of the editors' plans and approves of their principles of entry selection as being more sophisticated than those of _DA_. The review points out that, for compounds with _prairie_, _DCHP_ gives 11 new items, 2 new senses, and 1 antedating citation. For compounds with _Indian_, there are 4 antedatings and 30 new items. There is an antedating for _massassauga_ 'prairie rattler.' The review also notes 5 omissions.

439. __________. "Some Social Differences in Pronunciation," in _Contemporary English: Change and Variation_. Ed. David L. Shores (q.v.). p. 42-52.

This article describes and exemplifies 6 features of the pronunciation of CE.

440. __________. "Systematic Features with Social Significance in North American English." _Actes du Xe Congrès International des Linguistes_. Ed. A Grauer. Bucarest: Editions de l'Académie de la République Socialiste de Roumanie, 1969. I. p. 635-38.

This report of a paper notes, among its comments on AE, that in Newfoundland the three-way contrast of /b/, /v/, and /w/ is not always maintained.

441. __________. "Two Decades of the Linguistic Atlas." _JEGP_, 50 (1951), 101-10.

This article includes a brief account of fieldwork in the Maritimes completed at the date of writing.

McDavid, Raven I., Jr. Cont'd.

442. ________. "Why Do We Talk That Way?" [On title-page as "Why We Talk the Way We Do."]. CBC Times, 11-17 Feb. 1951, p. 2 and 8.

After noting a call to cows as common to AE and CE, this article laments the contemporary lag in Canadian dialectology. It lists 4 lexical Canadianisms, 3 lexical items which have spread south from CE into AE, and 3 items from Pennsylvania which have spread from AE to CE. It concludes that there is no essential linguistic boundary between southern Ontario and the contiguous parts of the United States.

443. ________, and Audrey R. Duckert, eds. Lexicography in English. Annals of the New York Academy of Sciences, No. 211. New York: The New York Academy of Sciences, 1973.

This collection includes items 131 and 599 of this Bibliography.

444. ________, and Virginia Glenn McDavid. "Grammatical Differences in the North-Central States." AS, 35 (1960), 5-19. Reprinted in A Various Language: Perspectives on American Dialects. Ed. Juanita V. Williamson and Virginia M. Burke (q.v.). p. 341-56.

This article notes that the Hudson Valley forms /wunt/, /wʊnt/ 'won't' are common in Ontario communities surveyed for the Linguistic Atlas of the North Central States.

445. ________, and ________. "h Before Semivowels in the Eastern United States." Language, 28 (1952), 41-62.

The maps in this article show whip, whetstone, wheelbarrow, whinney, and whoa as pronounced with initial /w/ in the Saint John Valley in New Brunswick, but with /hw/ thence to the U.S. border. Wharf has /w/ and humor has /j/ throughout all western New Brunswick. In 2 (unspecified) communities in southern Ontario, wheel has /w/, but wheelbarrow has /hw/.

446. ________, and ________. "Regional linguistic Atlases in the United States." Orbis, 5 (1956), 349-86.

This article includes an account of work done and in progress

McDavid, Raven I., Jr. Cont'd.

in 1956 on regional speech in Canada. Henry Alexander's fieldwork in the Maritimes, H. Rex Wilson's work in Queen's County, N.S., and the interest of the then newly formed CLA are all mentioned.

447. __________, and Sarah Ann Witham. "Poor Whites and Rustics." _Names_, 22 (1974), 93-103.

Although mainly concerned with AE, this article gives the terms obtained for rustics in 8 New Brunswick and 16 Ontario communities. In New Brunswick, the most popular term was _countryman_; 5 other terms were collected, 2 of them peculiar to the province. In Ontario, the most popular term was _backwoodsman_, with _hayseed_ and _hick_ sharing second place. The article records 11 other terms, 1 peculiar to the province.

448. McDougall, Robert L. Review of _A Dictionary of Canadianisms on Historical Principles_, Walter S. Avis, Ed.-in-Chief. _Canadian Geographical Journal_, 78:3 (Mar. 1969), 6 and 8.

This review of _DCHP_ first relates that work to _DA_, then shows how environment influences language, citing 2 examples of this. The reviewer adversely criticizes _DCHP_ on the grounds that some entries, e.g., that for _buggy_, do not supplement information already published; that there are some omissions, e.g., "responsible government"; that some etymologies, e.g., that of _shaman_, are not adequate; and that some entries, e.g., that for _shake_, give insufficient historical evidence.

449. McKeown, John A., ed. _The Canadian Teaching Dictionary for Junior Grades_. Toronto: Clarke, Irwin, 1961.

This dictionary contains 9,500 of the most commonly used words "not part of every child's vocabulary." The definitions aim at illustration as much as at verbal restatement. Each polysyllabic main entry is repeated in italics with syllable divisions and stress markings.

450. __________, ed. _A Dictionary for Young Canadians_. Toronto: Clarke, Irwin, 1962.

This is a reprint of _CTD_, q.v.

451. McKeown, Robert. "How Do You Pronounce 'Tomato'?" Weekend Magazine (Montreal), 5 June 1954, p. 8.

This article describes the activities and outlines the methods of a fieldworker in the Maritimes, quoting 8 of the worksheet items. Storing and processing of data are also mentioned, as is the relationship of this work to that done in the United States. The variety of dialect in the Maritimes is glanced at.

452. McLay, W.S.W. "A Note on Canadian English." AS, 5 (1930), 328-29.

Replying to "Montreal English" by Helen C. Munroe, q.v., this article denies the validity for "the ordinary speech of the common people" of 8 of that writer's choices from the pairs she cites for Montreal English.

453. McLean, John. The Indians, Their Manners and Customs. Toronto: William Briggs, 1889.

This book devotes p. 197-201 to listing "Western Americanisms" which had passed into the speech of western Canada. It gives 51 lexical items and 9 idioms with this provenance.

454. Mencken, H.L. The American Language. New York: Knopf, 1919. 2nd ed. Revised and Enlarged, 1921. 3rd ed. Revised and Enlarged, 1923. 4th ed. Corrected, Enlarged, and Rewritten, 1936.

The 1st edition of this work mentions Canadian conservatism in the use of the prefix Hon. (p. 120). As evidence of AE influence on CE, it instances CE's many borrowings from vulgate AE, its use of spellings in -or (for BE -our), and the prevalence of "flat a " (all p. 318). The 2nd edition repeats all 4 points (p. 140, 242, 382-83, and 216 respectively), adding that most so-called Canadianisms are really American (p. 383), and giving a 6-item bibliography of CE (p. 452-53). The same points appear in the 3rd edition (p. 141-42, 249, 392-93, 224, 292, and 463 respectively). The 4th edition repeats only the comments on the prefix Hon., on spellings, and on the "flat a " (p. 277, 338, and 396 respectively). It adds that while "General American" prevails in Canada west of Montreal, the dialect of New Brunswick and Nova Scotia (outside Halifax) resembles that of New England. Throughout Canada, AE vocabulary is dominant (p. 371). Where AE and BE clash, as in Canada, the former will ultimately dominate (p. 608-09).

Mencken, H.L. Cont'd.

455. __________. The American Language: Supplement I. New York: Knopf, 1945. Supplement II. 1948.

Supplement I again mentions the Canadian conservatism in the use of the prefix Hon. and notes the Canadian -or spellings (p. 545, and n.). Passim, it cites 10 examples of Canadian lexical usage and 3 of Canadian slang. It also gives 2 instances of CE invading AE. Supplement II, as well as commenting on BE spellings in CE (p. 286 and 316), on 3 features of Newfoundland speech (p. 357, 358, and 387), and on the speech of the Prairie Provinces (p. 127), gives an 8-page description of CE (p. 248-55). This briefly traces the history of scholarship on CE, then characterizes general CE as resembling AE, citing 3 phonological features and 3 lexical items to support this. The dialects of the Maritimes, Newfoundland, Labrador, and Lunenburg, N.S. are also described, with 74 lexical items, 6 phonological features, and 2 morphological items quoted for the first two; 12 lexical items and 1 syntactical item for the third; and 15 lexical items and 2 phonological features for the last.

456. __________. The American Language. Abridged, with Annotations and New Material, by Raven I. McDavid, Jr., with the assistance of D.W. Maurer. New York: Knopf, 1963.

Besides mentioning the CE use of Canuck (p. 368n), bluenose, and herring choker (p. 375n), and of 2 orthographies (p. 488n: 17 examples are given), this book (p. 469-71) outlines Canadian settlement patterns and notes, despite the continued influence of BE, the close resemblance of CE to AE. Ontario speech differs phonologically from neighbouring AE in only 2 features and the pronunciation of some words. The strong influence of New England on the Maritime speech is remarked, as are the dialects of Newfoundland and of Lunenburg, N.S., of which 9 lexical items and 1 phonological feature are cited.

457. Meredith, Mamie. "Notes on American Weather Terms." AS, 6 (1931), 466.

This cites the note "'Squaw Winter,' 'Indian Winter,' 'Dogwood Winter'" by W.J. Wintemberg, q.v., as evidence for the use in Canada of the term squaw winter for an April snowfall.

458. Merriman, Alec. "Special Dictionary for Canadians." Daily Colonist (Victoria, B.C.), 26 Mar. 1967, p. 14.

This review of SD gives its place in the DCE series, notes its founding in research, and records the names of its editorial board. The review exemplifies 10 Canadianisms whose inclusion in SD shows how it displaces British and American dictionaries for use by Canadians. It gives 6 examples of variation in CE spelling and 4 of variation in pronunciation, and it indicates that SD gives alternatives in both areas. Finally, it gives 10 examples to show SD's lexical contemporaneity and 4 to show its phrasal comprehensiveness.

459. Mifflen, J.B. "Around Newfoundland With a Lexicon." Ontario Library Review, 40 (1956), 226-28.

This article describes 1 phonological and 1 morphological feature of Newfoundland speech and gives 78 examples of words and phrases common in, and more or less peculiar to, Newfoundland. The article is loosely organized round a fictional account of life in that province.

460. Millais, J.G. "Some Newfoundland Colloquialisms," in Newfoundland and Its Untrodden Ways. London: Longmans, 1907. p. 338-39.

After a brief note relating Newfoundland dialect to its English West Country origins, this article records and defines 26 Newfoundland words.

461. Mitchell, Bob. "Canadian Slang Will Get Dictionary." Victoria Daily Times (Victoria, B.C.), 28 Dec. 1968, p. 12.

This article on the then proposed dictionary of Canadian slang includes the meanings and attributed derivations of some of the slang words in CE.

462. Moon, Barbara. "Does Anybody Here Speak Canadian?" Maclean's Magazine, 2 June 1962, p. 24-25 and 50-51.

This humorous, journalistic review of DCCD cites 20 words noted by that dictionary as Canadianisms. It quotes, but doubts the Canadianism of, a further 12. Another 11 words thought by the reviewer to be Canadian are not so marked, and another 24 are not in the dictionary at all. The reviewer cites 1 alleged misdefinition.

463. Moore, Mavor. "How We Talk Canadian." SatN, Nov. 1967, p. 54-55.

This review of DCHP cites 5 words exemplifying DCHP's criterion of Canadianism. A further 5 examples show etymological variety, DCHP's contribution to national identity, and Canada's contribution to international vocabulary. Other topics mentioned are French influence on CE, the Canadian aptitude at exchanging parts of speech, DCHP's value as a history sourcebook, and the cultural areas producing Canadianisms. DCHP's indifference to evidence from dramatic works, and its lack of dialectal pronunciations, lead the reviewer to call DCHP more glossary than dictionary.

464. Moreton, Rev. Julian. "Words and Phrases Peculiar to Newfoundland," in Life and Work in Newfoundland. London: Rivingtons, 1863, p. 29-51.

This work records 10 phonological items, 4 random pronunciations, and 89 lexical items observed by the author in Newfoundland in the mid-nineteenth century.

465. Morris, Lois. "Are You 'Neat' or 'Fink'? Teen Slang Pegs Everyone." Albertan (Calgary), 3 Mar. 1964, p. 9.

This article cites 39 expressions current among Calgary teenagers, defining or illustrating each. It lists also 1 morphological item.

466. Mott, Lewis F. "Items from Newfoundland." DN, 5 (1926), 406.

This article lists and defines 4 expressions noted by the author in Torbay, Nfld., in 1909.

467. __________ (as reported by Percy W. Long). "Canada." DN, 4 (1916), 332.

This article lists and defines 5 lexical items from Newfoundland and quotes Professor Mott's opinion that "there is much interesting material in those islands which their comparative isolation has preserved."

468. Munroe, Helen C. "Montreal English." AS, 5 (1930), 21.

This article lists 26 lexical and 2 phonological items in which the CE spoken in Montreal differs from AE. (For a criticism of this, see item 452 of this Bibliography.)

469. __________. "Profitunity." AS, 6 (1930-1931), 394.

This article notes the appearance of the blend profitunity in the Montreal Gazette of 4 Feb. 1931.

470. __________. "'Raise' or 'Rise'?" AS, 6 (1930-1931), 407-10.

On the basis of cited correspondence between a Montreal coke company and its customers, this article speculates on the currency of raise as 'salary increment' in CE.

471. Murray, Brenda. "G-Deletion in Canadian Dialects of English." CWPL, 1:1 (1975), 39-43.

This article discusses and, with the aid of 21 examples, attempts to formulate a rule to explain why [ŋ], [ŋg], and [ŋk] differ in their domains in 2 (unspecified) dialects of CE.

472. Nekrassov, Vladimir. "The Trickcyclist: Ein Glossar der Sprache der amerikanischen und kanadischen Rauschgiftsüchtigen." LSp, 19 (1974), 161-70.

The author states that the vocabulary of drug abuse is uniform throughout North America. He then gives and glosses, in English and German, 1,061 terms from that vocabulary. Only 1, however, brown rine 'heroin,' is specified as "chiefly in Canada."

473. Nelson, C.D. Review of The Senior Dictionary. Ed. Walter S. Avis and others. B.C. Teacher (Vancouver), 7:3 (Dec. 1967), 132.

This review of SD notes its character as being neither too British nor too American. It quotes SD's view of CE as being a blend of BE and AE.

474. Nicholson, Brian. "Pure BBC Accent Is Handicap Here, English Girl Finds." Telegram (Toronto), 22 July, 1953, p. 1 and 4.

This article deals primarily with the problems which her accent posed for an English speaker of RSE in Canada. Incidentally, it reports Canadians as saying "Toronna" and "Sarrurday".

475. Norman, Ella L. "The Norman Review." Argus (Official Publication of the Public School Trustees' Association of Ontario), 21:4 (Apr. 1962), 151.

This article reviews BD and CTD in separate paragraphs. The review of BD notes its place in DCE and notes that DCE is based on CE, not AE or BE. It mentions the grade-orientation of BD and praises its explanatory technique. The review of CTD mentions the purpose of the work, notes the number of entries therein, and lauds, giving 1 example, its method of defining words.

476. [North, John.] "This Corrupt Dialect." EngQ, 5:3 (Fall, 1972), 5-8.

This article notes 1 item of Canadian pronunciation and 1 of syntax, and comments on 2 lexical, 2 grammatical, and 3 phonological items from the SCE.

477. Noseworthy, Ronald G. "A Dialect Survey of Grand Bank, Newfoundland." M.A. thesis. Memorial Univ. of Newfoundland, 1971.

This thesis is based on responses from 21 informants selected in accordance with LAUSC principles. The chapter on phonemes lists and discusses each phoneme and its allophones, and identifies characteristics common to all informants. The chapter on syntax deals with parts of speech and their dialectal variants. The next chapter deals with selected lexical items. The last chapter discusses idiolect-forming factors. Appendices give, among other things, the informants' biographies. There is a glossary of 1,101 local words and phrases.

478. __________. "Fishing Supplement--Newfoundland Dialect Questionnaire." RLS, No. 5 (21 Jan. 1974), p. 18-21.

This supplement adds 96 items, specified in this article, to the Newfoundland questionnaire already developed. Some demand more than a single-word response.

Noseworthy, Ronald G. Cont'd.

479. ________. "Verb Usage in Grand Bank." RLS, No. 4 (1 May 1972), p. 19-24.

Based on part of the author's M.A. thesis, q.v., this study records the local variants of the present and past tenses of to be, its frequent lack of concord with plural nouns, the use of bees (vb.), of been without have, and of idden for is not. The forms of 6 other verbs, the use of participial a-, and the lack of concord with do and other verbs are also noted. The author cites 7 dialect nouns which occur also as verbs.

480. O'Brien, R.A. "Good and Bad Authorities." Kingston Whig-Standard, 26 Oct. 1963, p. 4.

This review objects to ID because it gives "American" spellings before "British," of which the review gives 1 example. It also objects to ID's claim to represent the usage of educated Canadians on the grounds that its usage differs from that of the author of the review and of his colleagues.

481. ________. "The poverty of Canadian English." Canadian Commentator, 5 (1961), 22-23.

The author objects to certain characteristics of CE, mainly the Americanization of some of its spellings, of which he gives 2 examples. He also objects to some changes of meaning, giving 1 example; to some usages, giving 1 example; and to some compound words, giving 6 examples.

482. Orkin, Mark M. Canajan, Eh? Don Mills, Ont.: General Publishing, 1973.

This humourous book records 282 words and phrases purportedly from CE, in quasi-phonetic spelling. Some entries are accompanied by short essays on Canadiana, partly in normal, partly in quasi-phonetic spelling.

483. [________.] "Canajan From A to Z." Reader's Digest, Mar. 1974, p. 59-62.

This condensation gives 25 entries, some abbreviated, from Canajan, Eh? by Mark M. Orkin.

Orkin, Mark M. Cont'd.

484. ________. Speaking Canadian English: An Informal Account of the English Language in Canada. Toronto: General Publishing, 1970.

After an introduction outlining early scholarship on CE, a chapter on the "hallmarks" of CE notes some of the outstanding characteristics of that form of speech. The next chapter gives the historical origins of CE, and the next deals with its ingredients: Canadianisms, Americanisms, and Briticisms; Indian, Eskimo, Gaelic and German; Newfoundland English; and Chinook Jargon. Later chapters deal with pronunciation, spelling and syntax, names, slang, and the future of Canadian English. There is a bibliography of 289 items.

485. ________. Speaking Canadian French: An Informal Account of the French Language in Canada. Toronto: General Publishing, 1967. Rev. 1971.

The section on the influence of Canadian French on CE cites 10 pre-nineteenth century loans, a further 5 from the Northwest Territories, and 6 more referring to fauna, farming, etc.

486. Orrell, John. "Canadianisms." Beaver, 302:3 (Winter 1971), 20-22.

This article describes the physical differences between the first and second editions of the Western Canadian Dictionary and Phrase Book by John Sandilands, q.v. It comments on the difference in character of the content of the two editions and quotes 10 entries from the later edition. (Through no fault of Orrell's, the second edition of Sandilands' work is herein wrongly dated as 1912 instead of 1913.)

487. Paddock, Harold J. "The Destruction of Language in Newfoundland." Morning Watch, 2:2 (Jan. 1975), 1-3.

Protesting against the schools' denigration of non-standard speech, the author records and exemplifies 6 phonological features and 1 morphological feature of Newfoundland dialect.

488. ________. "A Dialect Survey of Carbonear, Newfoundland." M.A. thesis. Memorial Univ. of Newfoundland, 1966.

This thesis is based on interviews with 24 informants. The principles of informant selection are described, as is the

Paddock, Harold J. Cont'd.

questionnaire used. The thesis then presents some notes on the grammar of the area studied, and gives phonetic impressions and a phonemic analysis of the speech. The vocabulary is also examined. Finally, the linguistic variations found are correlated with socio-economic and other differences.

489. ________. "The Folk Grammar of Carbonear, Newfoundland," in Canadian English: Origins and Structures. Ed. J.K. Chambers (q.v.). p. 25-32.

This is a reprint of Chapter 1 of "A Dialect Study of Carbonear, Newfoundland" by the same author, q.v.

490. Paikeday, Thomas M., ed. The Compact Dictionary of Canadian English. Toronto: Holt, Rinehart and Winston of Canada, 1970. Reprinted 1976.

This is the paperback edition of The Winston Dictionary of Canadian English. Intermediate edition. Ed. Thomas M. Paikeday, q.v.

491. ________. "English Usage." Letter to the editor. Globe and Mail (Toronto), 23 May 1974, p. 6.

This defends the word ethnicity, as having been in use in CE since 1971, as the author's own lexicographical files show.

492. ________, ed. The Winston Dictionary of Canadian English. Intermediate edition. Toronto: Holt, Rinehart and Winston of Canada, 1969. Reprinted 1970.

According to its Preface (p. vi), this dictionary contains about 65,000 vocabulary entries. Also, "other salient features . . . are the inclusion of usage notes and hundreds of items of Canadian English vocabulary as well as usage."

493. ________, ed. The Winston Dictionary of Canadian English. Elementary Edition. Toronto: Holt, Rinehart and Winston of Canada, 1975.

According to its preface (p. vi), this dictionary contains about 30,000 vocabulary entries under 20,000 headwords.

It includes 100 "word studies." Of these, the dictionary says: "The vast majority of the word studies are Canadiana."

494. Palmer, Francis W. "Gleanings for the DAE Supplement." AS, 22 (1947), 199-206.

After commenting on the etymological interest of Haliburton's use of A-No. 1, graft, and spile in The Clockmaker, this article gives 6 words from DAE which can be antedated from The Clockmaker and a further 9 which are in The Clockmaker but not in DAE.

495. Palmer, P.E. "By Any Other Name." Canadian Geographical Journal, 36 (1948), 149-51.

This article shows how a variety of different words may be used to denote similar physical features. The author gives 12 groups of words, each group denoting only 1 physical feature; some notes are added on the geographical variation within some of the groups. Conversely, 2 words, creek and island, may denote different things in different parts of Canada.

496. Parsons, Edward. "Dictionary's Errors Approved by Education Department." Globe and Mail (Toronto), 19 May 1962, p. 19.

While this review of A Dictionary for Young Canadians, ed. John A. McKeown, accepts some of its definitions as neat, many are held to be poor in content or style, 13 examples being given. Inconsistencies in entry selection are shown by 10 examples, and the reviewer specifies 17 errors in the accentuation guide and 9 in syllabication. He also remarks on 3 inadequacies in the pronunciation guide, 1 of them being exemplified. The dictionary contains 9 misspellings, of which 3 are quoted.

497. Parton, Lorne. "The Written Word." Province (Vancouver), 23 Mar. 1967, p. 5.

Quoting 5 lexical items from SD, this review implies its value for Canadian identity. It gives the total number of SD's entries and gives 2 examples of the Canadian pronunciations it records. The review draws attention to the several Canadian regional accents, and 2 Canadian pronunciations are given. Finally, 2 orthographical and 2 lexical examples show CE as an amalgam of BE and AE.

498. Partridge, Eric. "Canada," in Slang Today and Yesterday. London: Routledge and Kegan Paul. 4th rev. ed. 1970. p. 292-94.

Although he acknowledges that some Canadian slang exists and quotes 36 examples of Canadian soldiers' slang from the First World War, the author holds that it is "80 per cent American " and approves Mencken's theory that this is owing to the circulation in Canada of news from the American press agencies.

499. __________. A Dictionary of Slang and Unconventional English. 5th ed. 2 vols. London: Routledge and Kegan Paul, 1961. Reprinted 1963.

This dictionary contains some Canadian material, and the author acknowledges help from "Mr. Douglas Leechman and Professor F.E.L. Priestley of Canada" (p. ix).

500. __________. A Dictionary of the Underworld, British and American. London: Routledge and Kegan Paul, 1949. [Actually published 1950.]

This contains some Canadian material culled from "the leading newspaper in Toronto " (p. ix).

501. Paterson, Jack. "Let Us Not Be Mizzled!" Weekend Magazine, 20 Apr. 1963, p. 18 and 20.

This article gives 90 examples, said to have been collected from local radio stations across Canada, of words mispronounced or misread by the broadcasters.

502. __________. "Let's stamp out all this correct pronunciation." Maclean's Magazine, 13 Aug. 1960, p. 6.

This article records, in quasi-phonetic spelling, 11 CE pronunciations characterized as non-standard.

503. Patterson, Rev. George. "Notes on the Dialect of the People of Newfoundland." JAF, 8 (1895), 27-40.

Based on the author's observation, this article records 141 Newfoundland words and expressions, of which 61 are classified as survivals of words elsewhere obsolete, 37 as words used in senses uncommon elsewhere, and 43 as miscellaneous words of unknown origin. Some information on pronunciation (12 examples), morphology (14 examples),

Patterson, Rev. George. Cont'd.

syntax (3 features), and usage (9 items) is also given.

504. ________. "Notes on the Dialect of the People of Newfoundland: II." JAF, 9 (1896), 19-37.

From various sources other than his personal observation, the author gives further information concerning 9 of the items in his "Notes on the Dialect of the People of Newfoundland," q.v. He adds a further 140 items to the total. The words are classified in a manner similar to that used in the previous article. Some further information on pronunciation (4 examples) and on usage (18 examples) is likewise included. Also noted is the occurrence of tickle (tittle) in Nova Scotia and New Brunswick.

505. ________. "Notes on the Dialect of the People of Newfoundland: III." JAF, 10 (1897), 203-13.

In this article, the author lists, unclassified and in alphabetical order, 70 words (including 4 already mentioned in his two earlier articles on this topic, q.v.) from Newfoundland speech. The list includes 6 examples of Newfoundland pronunciations and 16 items of usage.

506. ________. "Notes on the Dialect of the People of Newfoundland." Proceedings and Transactions of the Nova Scotian Institute of Science, 9 [= N.S. 2] (1896), xliv-lxxvii.

Apart from its notes on foreright, midered, idle, varket, farl, and a scattered one, this article offers mainly a selection of the material in this author's first two articles of the same title. Most of this article is verbatim quotation from these earlier works.

507. Pei, Mario. The Story of English. Philadelphia: J.B. Lippincott, 1952.

This author regards CE, which he treats very briefly, as "quite homogeneous " and as very like AE. In support of this latter assertion, he cites an otherwise unidentified "British-compiled Dictionary of Canadianisms containing approximately one thousand terms" of which "only about three dozen are found which are not common in the United States as well " (p. 158).

Pei, Mario. Cont'd.

508. ________. The Story of the English Language. New York: Simon and Schuster, 1967.

This is a revision of The Story of English by the same author, q.v. The material on CE is virtually unchanged.

509. Pennington, Bob. "Expert can pinpoint your accent." Toronto Star, 27 Mar. 1974, p. E2.

This article draws attention to the large number of accents in Toronto and throughout the rest of Canada. CE as a distinct regional variety of English is evidenced by the word grippe, used in Canada though not nowadays in Britain.

510. [Percy, H.R.] "The IZE Age." CAB, 41:3 [Spring 1966], inside front cover and p. 1.

This article objects to the growing use of the suffix -ize and gives 5 examples of objectionable words formed therewith. The author gives reasons for his point of view and speculates about the causes of the phenomenon.

511. Peters, Robert D. "The Social and Economic Effects of the Transition from a System of Woods Camps to a System of Commuting in the Newfoundland Pulpwood Industry." M.A. thesis. Memorial Univ. of Newfoundland, 1965.

This thesis includes, on p. 201-07, a glossary of 63 items used by lumbermen in Newfoundland.

512. Phelan, E.C. "On Guard for English." Imperial Oil Review, 59:4 (1975), 20-23.

While agreeing that language changes, the author attacks as errors 29 innovations in CE but accepts 5 others. He laments the passing of 5 Canadianisms and urges the retention of 6 others. Finally, he notes the disagreement among the usage authorities regarding as if and as though.

513. Počeptsov, G.G. Review of A Dictionary of Canadianisms on Historical Principles, Walter S. Avis, Ed.-in-Chief. Movoznavstvo (Linguistics), No. 2 (Mar.-Apr. 1970), p. 92-94. (Pub. by the Ukrainian Academy of Sciences).

This review mentions DCHP's importance for the study of

regional English. It notes the inadequacy for CE of other dictionaries and summarizes the history of DCHP, whose criteria of Canadianism it praises, giving 5 examples. DCHP's derivations are approved as indicating the importance of Indian and Eskimo languages, 6 and 4 examples being given respectively, and as displaying the results of false etymology, as 2 examples show. The reviewer cites 13 examples which show the importance of French influence, while 3 show Canadian changes of RSE and 4 show Slavic influence.

514. Poelzer, Big Al. Hippy Dictionary. [? Vancouver]: Dollina, 1970.

Printed in Canada, this work defines, in more or less alphabetical order, 156 words from the argot of the "hippies."

515. Pope, Sir Joseph. Memoirs of Sir John A. Macdonald. Ottawa: Durie, [1894] II. p. 268 and 349.

This records Sir John A. Macdonald's firm adherence to the BE spelling practice, quoting his Minute of Council, q.v., as evidence.

516. Porter, Bernard H. "A Newfoundland Vocabulary." AS, 38 (1963), 297-301.

This is an almost verbatim repetition of 169 of the items from the same author's article of the same title in Northeast Folklore, q.v. A few illustrative quotations are added.

517. ________. "A Newfoundland Vocabulary." Northeast Folklore, 3 (1960), 35-39.

This lists and glosses 176 Newfoundland words. The list and the glosses are almost identical with those in Historic Newfoundland by L.E.F. English, q.v., as is noted in "Bibliography of Writings on Newfoundland English" [by William J. Kirwin], q.v.

518. ________. "Some Newfoundland Phrases, Sayings, and Figures of Speech." AS, 41 (1966), 294-97.

This records 143 Newfoundland phrases, 85 of which appear in Historic Newfoundland by L.E.F. English, q.v. The other 58 contain a few words apparently peculiar to Newfoundland.

519. Preston, Donald. "Canadian Slang." M.A. thesis. Univ. of Victoria, Victoria, B.C., 1973.

The author compared 4,306 lexical items, including 3,300 entries from the files of the Lexicographical Centre of the University of Victoria, with the entries in _A Dictionary of Slang and Unconventional English_ by Eric Partridge, _A Dictionary of Americanisms on Historical Principles_ by Mitford M. Mathews, and the _Dictionary of American Slang_ by Harold Wentworth and Stuart Berg Flexner. He found that 2,450 of his items were exclusively Canadian in use, while 2,128 were of Canadian origin.

520. Price, Mrs. Carl, and Clyde Kennedy. _Renfrew County_. Pembroke, Ont.: Renfrew County Council, 1961.

Under the heading "Valley Speech," the authors include 2 examples of words adopted from Amerindian via French into Ottawa Valley English and 1 of borrowing directly from French. The local pronunciation of Fr. _oiseau_ (in a place name) as "weesa" is also noted.

521. Priestley, F.E.L. "Canadian English," in _British and American English Since 1900_. Ed. Eric Partridge and John W. Clark. New York: Philosophical Library, 1951. Reprinted New York: Greenwood, 1968. p. 72-79.

After a brief outline of the relevant Canadian settlement history, the author claims a recently developed basic homogeneity for CE and speculates that the national self-confidence of Canadians will safeguard this speech from Americanization. Various factors which have helped to maintain a partial linguistic independence for Canada are listed.

522. ________. "Do We Talk 'Canadian'?" _SatN_, 10 May 1952, p. 13.

After noting 10 features of pronunciation without giving details of Canadian practice, the author proposes that the speech of the "best C.B.C. announcers" be adopted as a standard. He points out that this form of speech originates in Canadian settlement history, and he describes CE as relatively more homogeneous than AE. Contact with BE in education and in other fields has made Canadians bi-dialectal in AE and BE. The author gives 12 examples of the truth of this and notes the value of cultural hybridization.

Priestley, F.E.L. Cont'd.

523. __________. "English Language [in Canada]." Encyclopedia Canadiana. Toronto: Grolier of Canada, 1957. IV. p. 8-11.

The author characterizes CE as more homogeneous than AE, which it partly resembles. This is shown by 8 phonological features (all exemplified), although the features are less marked in CE than in AE. The inter-cultural situation allows Canadians to understand more Americanisms than they use. Similarly, CE includes many Americanisms (18 examples) and many Briticisms (6 examples), but the former probably preponderate. The author cites 34 examples to show Amerindian or Eskimo influence, 13 to show French, and 8 to show native Canadianisms. In spelling, 19 examples show CE as an amalgam of AE and BE.

524. Pumphrey, Ronald. Strange Facts About Newfoundland. St. John's, Nfld.: Guardian, [1952].

Quoting an unspecified article from the Montreal Gazette, the author repeats, on p. 7, the claim that Newfoundland's outports preserve Elizabethan English and cites 7 Elizabethan words surviving in Newfoundland speech.

525. Rawlings, W.H. Letter to the editor. Verbatim, 2:2 (Sept. 1975), 16.

This evidences the use in Canada of barberchair (vb.) 'twist around' in lumbering slang, although the word is apparently an Americanism.

526. Reader's Guide for New Canadians. Toronto: Globe and Mail, [c. 1958].

This glossary lists 205 words, phrases, and abbreviations commonly used in the Toronto Globe and Mail and explains each in English, German, Italian, and Dutch.

527. Rempel, Rosemary. "An Introduction to Trisyllabic Laxing, Vowel Shift, and Canadian Raising." CWPL, 1:1 (1975), 3-7.

This article uses 23 examples to formulate a rule explaining the alternation between [ɨ] and [ʌ] in trisyllabic words on the one hand, and [ay] and [aw], respectively, in related words on the other. The rule stated in "Canadian Raising" by J.K.

Chambers, q.v., is invoked to explain the similar alternation between [ay], [aw] and [ʌy], [ʌw].

528. Robertson, Strowan. "More Canadians Are Gulled by Advertisers than Any Other Brand." Canadian Art 77, 19 (1962), 347.

This article takes issue with the English of 4 television commercials; the author claims that errors violate clarity and accuracy of communication.

529. Rodman, Lilita. "Characteristics of B.C. English." EngQ, 7:4 (Winter 1974/1975), 49-82.

This article first explains that the SCE responses for British Columbia were sorted into 3 groups: Vancouver Island, Greater Vancouver, and Mainland B.C. It then describes in detail the processing of the response figures and states the criteria for significance. Its conclusions are: that Vancouver Island dialect is unique in British Columbia in 5 phonological, 4 grammatical, and 4 lexical items; that Greater Vancouver is similarly unique in 11 phonological, 8 grammatical, and 7 lexical items; and that Mainland B.C. is similarly unique in 3 phonological and 4 lexical items.

530. Rogers, P.W. "Unlocking the Canadian Word Hoard." QQ, 77 (1970), 111-23.

This article first compares SD with WI. Both are equally good in vocabulary, definitions, usage labels, and guides. WI has clearer principles of selection and a better phonological notation. SD gives a better selection of Canadian slang and is more realistic on variant spellings and regional pronunciations. The article then reviews DCHP. Its history is outlined, and its purpose and doctrine of Canadianisms are quoted. The high proportion of place names among the Canadianisms is exemplified, and the entries under Canada are discussed. DCHP's evidencing of the regionalized character of the Canadian vocabulary is mentioned. Much of the vocabulary in DCHP is noted to be disappearing. DCHP is praised for its illustrations, phonemicizations, etymologies, and citations.

531. Ross, Mary Lowrey. "Exploration in Depth." SatN, 18 Feb. 1961, p. 38.

This article records and comments, not always favorably, on 13 words and phrases which had then recently achieved currency in CE.

532. Roth, Ruth S. "The Relevance of Morpheme Boundaries to Nasal Assimilation in Canadian English." CWPL, 1:1 (1975), 37-38.

This article uses 29 examples, from the author's own idiolect and elsewhere, to refine the rule stated in Sound Pattern of English by Noam Chomsky and Morris Halle (New York: Harper and Row, 1968), p. 419. She contends that morpheme divisions account for some non-velar realizations of /n/.

533. Rouleau, Ernest. "Some Newfoundland Vernacular Plant Names." Studies on the Vascular Flora of the Province of Newfoundland (Canada)-II. Contributions de l'Institut Botanique de l'Université de Montréal, No. 69. Montréal: Institut Botanique de l'Univ. de Montréal, 1956.

This article gives 242 vernacular plant names current in Newfoundland; 42 of them are marked as having a Newfoundland meaning different from the meaning they have elsewhere in Canada.

534. Rowe, Nora Alice (Crittenden). "A Linguistic Study of the Lake Ainslie Area of Inverness County, Nova Scotia." M.A. thesis. Louisiana State University in New Orleans, 1968.

This study is based on the LAUSC project. Its phonological material discusses 14 stressed vowels and 7 consonants and their variants. It includes a summary of morphological and syntactic responses (58 items) and of vocabulary responses (107 items). There are chapters on the method of the study and on the economics of the area. Appendices give the worksheet, the informants' biographies, and an index of features.

535. Roy, Rev. James. Law in Language: A Thesis. Montreal: "Witness," 1883.

In a treatise mainly theoretical and comparative, the author gives evidence for the existence in CE of 4 idioms and of the pronunciations "rheumatiz" and "neuralagi."

536. Rudnyckyj, J.B. "'Sputnik' and its Derivatives in North American English." PLCMND, 1 (1959), 27-28.

This article comments on sputnik and its derivatives in CE and AE, without, however, distinction being made between the two varieties of English.

537. Ruttan, Susan. "Archaic English: It's Alive Among the Kids." Victoria Times (Victoria, B.C.), 3 Oct. 1972, p. 17.

This article briefly describes the SCE and exemplifies 1 phonological item, 1 morphological item, and 2 idiomatic items from its findings. It also quotes, as M.H. Scargill's conclusion, the contention that "young people, having a more primitive, a more natural connection with the culture than adults have, may also have a 'feeling' for the appropriateness of some of the older forms of the language."

538. [Sabine, Lorenzo. Lecture on the Fisheries.] Quoted in "Report on the Fisheries in the Bay of Fundy" by Moses Henry Perley. Journal of the House of Assembly of the Province of New Brunswick from the Sixth Day of February to the Thirtieth Day of April 1851. Fredericton: Queen's Printer, 1851. Appendix, p. cxlvi-cxlvii. Reprinted in Reports on the Sea and River Fisheries of New Brunswick by M.H. Perley. Fredericton: Queen's Printer, 1852. p. 113-14.

This lecture gives 28 lexical items, 3 idioms, and 1 local variant in quasi-phonetic spelling, all from the speaker's observation of the speech of fishermen in the Bay of Fundy.

539. Sagi, Douglas. "You Can Tell Them by their Tongue." Globe Magazine, Toronto, 27 Sept. 1969, p. 2.

This article asserts that most areas in Canada have a regional speech. In quasi-phonetic spelling,'Trawna"is cited; Mr. Don Harron is said to exemplify Parry Sound, Ont., speech, and the Hon. Mr. Joe Green that of the Ottawa Valley. South of Calgary, the influence of AE is said to be strong, while the speech of Medicine Hat resembles Texan. In Saskatchewan, "dropping the g's," slurring, and frequent use of "Well, say," are all said to be common.

540. Sandilands, John. Western Canadian Dictionary and Phrase-Book. Winnipeg: Telegram Job Printers, 1912.

This edition gives 853 words and phrases in use in CE. Most, although not all, of the entries are serious in mood and purpose. The work includes many slang expressions, although it does not give usage labels.

Sandilands, John. Cont'd.

541. __________. Western Canadian Dictionary and Phrase-Book. Winnipeg: Telegram Job Printers [1913]. Reprinted with an Introduction by John Orrell. Edmonton, Alta.: Univ. of Alberta, 1978.

Advertised at "2 Bits or 1 Shinplaster Or 25 Cents " and claiming to be "The First Dictionary Ever Printed In Canada," this edition starts with a partial list of contents, consisting of facetious sayings, etc., each equated with its entry. There are about 1,530 entries, many of them not entirely serious. As in the 1912 edition, q.v., many slang expressions are included, although not so labelled.

542. Sandwell, B.K. "School-Teacher English." SatN, 19 Nov. 1938, p. 3.

This reply to "Toronto Writer Equally Culpable" by Francis J. MacNamara, q.v., defends the expressions attacked therein.

543. Saunders, Robert. "Glossary," in A Glimpse of Newfoundland (as it was and as it is) in Poetry and Pictures by Solomon Samson. Poole, England: J. Looker, 1959. p. 76-78.

This glossary gives 30 items in all; however, 6 of them are place or personal names, and only a few of the remainder are not in general use. For 12 of the entries, illustrative quotations are given from RSE authors.

544. __________. "Glossary," in A Glimpse of Newfoundland (as it was and as it is) in Poetry and Pictures by Solomon Samson. Poole, England: J. Looker, 1963. p. 76-81.

In this edition, there are an additional 10 items in the glossary. However, 3 are proper names, or abbreviations thereof, while another 4 are illustrated by quotations from RSE writing.

545. Scargill, M.H. "Canadian Dictionary Projects." Education (Toronto), 3 (1960), 79-87.

This is a reprint of "Canadian Dictionary Projects II: Canadian English" by M.H. Scargill, q.v.

Scargill, M.H. Cont'd.

546. ________. "Canadian Dictionary Projects II: Canadian English." META: Journal des Traducteurs-Translators' Journal, 3 (1958), 114-21.

This article describes the DCE project and discusses the various criteria available for dictionaries of Canadianisms. Among the criteria finally selected were: English words and phrases with meanings peculiar to Canada (3 examples); loans from Amerindian languages (6 examples), from French (2 examples), and from elsewhere (8 examples); and words originating in Canada (3 examples), including place names and nicknames (14 examples). The article ends by describing how evidential quotations will be amassed.

547. ________. "Canadian English." Letter to the editor. Edmonton Journal, 11 Apr. 1957, p. 4.

This rejoinder to "A Canadian Language?" Anon., q.v., argues that the very qualities that the citations in that article possess which convinced its author that a Canadian dictionary was not needed, are the same qualities which, in fact, make such a dictionary necessary.

548. ________. "Canadian English and Canadian Culture in Alberta." JCLA, 1, No. 1, Regular Series (Mar. 1955), 26-29.

After emphasizing the importance of language as a determinant of culture, the author carefully describes his method of investigating Alberta pronunciation. He describes the results in terms of "American," "British," and "free" pronunciations, citing the percentage of each in each quarter and in 6 cities of the province. He concludes that the "British" style of pronunciation will gradually yield to the American.

549. ________. "Canadianisms from Western Canada with Special Reference to British Columbia." PTRSC, 4th Series, Vol. 6 (1968), Sec. II, p. 181-85.

This article shows how CE reflects Canadian history. Its general differentiation from BE is exemplified in 12 lexical items and its regional variation in 3. Making special reference to British Columbia and its English, the author gives 9 examples of eponymy, 15 of words from Amerindian (including Chinook Jargon), and 27 of words derived from other important elements in western life and culture. The article ends with a plea for more support for the study of regional speech.

Scargill, M.H. Cont'd

550. __________. "Canadians Speak Canadian." SatN, 8 Dec. 1956, p. 16-18.

After producing 9 lexical examples to refute the claim that CE does not exist, the author exemplifies its variety and laments the then lack of scholarly works on CE, especially the lack of dictionaries and of usage-based grammars. The history of CE is mentioned, and its relation to and simultaneous independence of AE and BE are exemplified in 2 phonological features. Finally, the author notices the large Canadian lexicon, instancing 36 lexical items, and he gives 19 examples of the indifference with which contemporary dictionaries treat this lexicon.

551. __________. "Le Développement de la langue anglaise au Canada," in Histoire littéraire du Canada. Ed. Carl F. Klinck and others. Trans. Maurice Lebel. Quebec: Univ. Laval, 1970, p. 308-17.

This is a translation into French of "The Growth of Canadian English" by the same author, q.v.

552. __________. "Eighteenth-Century English in Nova Scotia." JCLA, 2, No. 1, Regular Series (Mar. 1956), 3.

Based on a study of the Original Minutes of His Majesty's Council at Annapolis Royal, 1720-1739, this article describes 4 features, supported by 6 examples, of the treatment of stressed vowels; 3 features, with 6 examples, of that of unstressed vocalics; 3 features, with 3 examples, of that of consonants; and 3 morphosyntactical features, with 3 examples. There are comparisons with the language of the Wentworth Papers, 1705-1739, and of the Verney Letters, 1696-1717.

553. __________. "The Growth of Canadian English," in Literary History of Canada. Ed. Carl F. Klinck and others. Toronto: Univ. of Toronto, 1965. p. 251-59; 2nd ed. Vol. I. 1976. p. 265-73.

After giving 45 examples of lexical items of CE, the author dates the earliest Canadian use of 44 Canadianisms. He cites 18 authors or works commenting on the Canadian lexicon, exemplifies the comments of each, and intersperses a note on the American, British, and Irish origins of various elements in Canadian phonology; he also cites the remarks of 4 writers who comment on Canadian pronunciation. He ends with a quotation in which Earle Birney describes his own attitude to CE.

Scargill, M.H. Cont'd.

554. _________. "Is Riz, Some Hot, Clumb, and Other Canadianisms." EngQ, 6:2 (Summer 1973), 115-21.

Based on the SCE, this article notes the increasing use by students of 2 phonological items, 1 lexical item, and 1 grammatical item obsolescent among their parents. The author cites 4 phonological items to show CE choosing AE forms, and 4 grammatical items to show other developments. He cites 2 lexical items and 1 phonological item to illustrate dialectal diversity, while 2 grammatical items, 1 lexical item, and 1 phonological item show the history of CE. He uses 6 grammatical items and 1 phonological item to relate CE to Sapir's drift hypothesis, while 2 grammatical and 2 phonological items show the choices CE is making.

555. _________. "Linguistics in Canada." Bulletin of the Humanities Association of Canada, No. 17 (1956), p. 2.

This article points to the independence of CE and cites 10 lexical examples to show that CE is misrepresented or ignored in contemporary dictionaries. The same is true of its spelling, pronunciation, and syntax. The author calls for a definitive study of CE.

556. _________. Modern Canadian English Usage: Linguistic Change and Reconstruction. Toronto: McClelland and Stewart in cooperation with the Canadian Council of Teachers of English, 1974.

Chapter 1 of this book outlines the significance of the SCE, whose primary aim was "to compare the speech of the younger generation with that of their parents." Chapters 2 through 5 give the results of 27 morphological, 42 phonological, 5 spelling, and 30 lexical questions. Each result is expressed as a table showing, by province and country-wide, the percentage of male parents, female parents, male students, and female students who gave each response. Each response is then characterized linguistically. Chapter 6 draws conclusions, and relates the SCE to the work of earlier linguists.

557. _________. "A Pilot Study of Alberta Speech: Vocabulary." JCLA, 1, No. 1 (Oct. 1954), 21-22.

After describing the method of the study and giving 2 samples from the questionnaire used, the author explains that the study was intended solely to show, as it did, the value of a complete linguistic survey of Alberta. The

Scargill, M.H. Cont'd.

author cites 16 definitions which produced responses varying with the age, location, etc., of the informants.

558. __________. "Sources of Canadian English." JEGP, 56 (1957), 610-14. Reprinted in Canadian English: Origins and Structures. Ed. J.K. Chambers (q.v.). p. 12-15.

This article advances several arguments to show that CE does not originate with the English of the Loyalists. It points out that the origins of CE are probably as many and various as its dialects.

559. __________. "Survey of Canadian English." Canadian Council of Teachers of English Newsletter, 3:3 (Fall 1970), 1 and 6.

This article explains the purpose and the mechanics of the SCE, illustrating with 3 examples the kind of linguistic variation it will examine. A pilot questionnaire of 20 items was circulated with the article.

560. __________. "Using the Historical Dictionary: A Concise Dictionary of Canadianisms." Speaking of Dictionaries, No. 2. Toronto: Gage Educational Publishing, n.d. n. pag.

After describing what a historical dictionary is, this article names 5 such and, using CDC as its source, cites 6 examples to show how a civilization adapts its language to new conditions and 9 to show how borrowed words are adapted to suit the structure of the borrowing language. Using the same source, the article cites a further 112 examples to show how the entries in CDC illustrate the history and culture of Canada.

561. __________, and Walter S. Avis. Review of The Structure of American English by W. Nelson Francis. JCLA, 6 (1960), 76-84.

In that part of the review which concerns CE, Walter S. Avis draws attention to the fact that /ow/ is the usual vowel of won't in CE, although /u/ may be heard in the Maritimes and occasionally elsewhere, and /ə/ in the St. Lawrence Valley. Also, CE uses live on King Street, not live in King Street.

Scargill, M.H. Cont'd.

562. __________, and P.G. Penner, eds. Looking at Language. Toronto: W.J. Gage, 1966. 2nd rev. ed. Glenview, Ill.: Scott, Foresman, 1969.

The first edition of this anthology contains items 117 and 632 of this Bibliography. The second contains only item 120.

563. __________, and H.J. Warkentyne. "The Survey of Canadian English: a Report." EngQ, 5:3 (Fall 1972), 47-104.

After a detailed description of the methodology of the SCE, this article tabulates the percentage of respondents (subclassified as male, female, parent, and student, by province and Canada-wide) giving each response to each question asked. Phonology occupies 42 such tables, grammar 28, vocabulary 29, and spelling 5. Each table is followed by a comment on the linguistic significance of each response. A brief conclusion deals with the results of the SCE as a whole.

564. Scharfe, Ruth E. "Ottawa Valley-ese." Ottawa Journal, Saturday Section, 26 Mar. 1966, p. 1.

The author records, in quasi-phonetic spelling, 56 words and phrases observed by her in the Ottawa Valley, though not all are from speakers native therein. She then makes some non-technical comment on the pronunciation of 13 words and on 5 phonological features of the speech of this area. Finally, she gives, again in quasi-phonetic spelling, a glossary of 48 regional items, including 7 already mentioned.

565. Scott, N.C. "kəneidiən caught ənd cot." Maître phonétique, 66:3 (1939), 22.

The writer reports that, in the speech of a Winnipeg informant, the vowel of caught has the same quality as the vowel of cot, but is distinguished from the latter by being longer. He adds that the same is true of the vowels of cawed and cod and asks if New England has a similar distinction.

566. Scott, S. Osborne. "The Red River Dialect," in Canadian English: Origins and Structures. Ed. J.K. Chambers (q.v.). p. 61-63.

This is a reprint of Part One of "The Red River Dialect" by S. Osborne Scott and D.A. Mulligan, q.v.

567. __________, and D.A. Mulligan. "The Red River Dialect." Beaver, 282 (Dec. 1951), 42-45.

In Part One of this article, Scott derives Red River dialect from Scottish English and Cree, pointing to the many Cree syntactical constructions the dialect contains. He advances the Cree's alleged difficulty with /l/ and /r/ and his inability to pronounce /š/ as a basis for some of its phonology. In Part Two, by Mulligan, 10 anecdotes and the story of Little Red Riding Hood, all in quasi-phonetic spelling, exemplify the dialect and record 7 loanwords from Amerindian. See also item *712 in the Addendum to this bibliography.

568. Scott, W.B. A Checklist of the Freshwater Fishes of Canada and Alaska. [Toronto]: Royal Ontario Museum, Division of Zoology and Palaeontology, 1958.

This checklist records the common names of 28 families and 198 species of fish, each listed under its scientific name. There is discussion of 9 of the names.

569. __________, and E.J. Crossman. The Freshwater Fishes of New Brunswick: A Checklist with Distributional Notes. Contributions of the Royal Ontario Museum, Division of Zoology and Palaeontology, No. 51. Toronto: [Royal Ontario Museum, Division of Zoology and Palaeontology], 1959.

This work lists the common and scientific names of 56 species of fish. Of the common names, 7 are italicized as indicating "New Brunswick usage."

570. Sčur, G.S. "Ob osobennostjax soslagatel'nogo naklonenija v angliskom jazyke Velikobritanii, SŠA, Avstralii i Kanady," in Voprosi teorii romano-germanskix jazykov. Vypusk 5, ed. S.S. Linskij. Dnepropetrovsk: Dnepropetrovskij ordena T.K.Z. gos. univ. im. 300 letija vossoedinenija Ukrainy s Rossiej, 1974.

(The authors could not obtain a copy of this before going to press.) The 1975 MLA International Bibliography, Volume III,

Linguistics notes (p. 112, #6440) "Subjunctive mood in Eng. lang. of Great Britain, USA, Australia, and Canada."

571. Seary, E.R., G.M. Story, and W.J. Kirwin. *The Avalon Peninsula of Newfoundland: An Ethno-Linguistic Study*. National Museum of Canada, Bulletin No. 219, Anthropological Series, No. 81. Ottawa: Queen's Printer, 1968.

After citing 68 lexical items, Part III of this work gives phoneme inventories of 5 Avalon Peninsula dialects: the "Southern Shoreline," "Northern Shoreline," Bay Roberts, St. John's cultivated, and St. John's folk. For the first dialect, extra, dental phonemes /t̪/ and /d̪/ are hypothesized. The second and third may lack /θ/ and /ð/, and the third /h/ as well. The third has an extra phoneme /a/. The vowel inventory of the fourth resembles that of RSE, while the last lacks /θ/, /ð/, and /a/. There are notes on the lexicon and grammar of the first dialect, and a hypothesis of the extensive survival of grammatical gender in the third. Possible developments are forecast.

572. Shores, David L., ed. *Contemporary English: Change and Variation*. Philadelphia: J.B. Lippincott, 1972.

This anthology contains items 437 and 439 of this *Bibliography*.

573. Smart, Reginald G., and David Jackson. *The Yorkville Subculture: A Study of the Life Styles and Interactions of Hippies and Non-Hippies*. Toronto: The Addiction Research Foundation, 1969.

The appendix to this work is a glossary of 186 words used by "hippies" in Toronto.

574. Smeaton, B. Hunter. Review of *A Bibliography of Writings on Canadian English (1857-1965)* by Walter S. Avis. *CJL*, 13 (1968), 129-30.

This review notes that of 126 entries in the work reviewed, only 16 appeared before 1900, and only 25 before 1930.

Smeaton, B. Hunter. Cont'd.

575. _________. Review of A Dictionary of Canadianisms on Historical Principles, Walter S. Avis, Ed.-in-Chief. LJ, 1 Apr. 1968, p. 1465.

This review of DCHP mentions the period covered by its entries and notes that each entry is substantiated by dated quotation. The size of DCHP's bibliography is specified and 9 examples are cited to show the semantic range of the entries. While some of its entries are undoubtedly common to AE and CE, DCHP is commended for its definition of a Canadianism.

576. Solomon, Hyman. "Canada Gets Own Dictionary." Toronto Daily Star, 21 Dec. 1959, p. 7.

After citing 2 words and 3 pronunciations showing CE as unique, this article mentions the inadequacy for CE of present dictionaries and describes the DCHP, then in preparation. A further 4 lexical and 3 phonological examples emphasize CE's uniqueness; 5 show words with a special significance in CE; and 6 show CE borrowing from Eskimo, Amerindian, and French. The author uses 6 phonological examples to differentiate CE from BE, and 4 to differentiate it from AE. The influences on CE are outlined, and the possible development of a standard is forecast. An illustration shows a page of the dictionary in preparation.

577. Southerland, Ronald, ed. "Readings on Language in Canada." Rev. ed. Mimeographed. Calgary: Univ. of Calgary, 1973.

This anthology includes items 130, 178, 289, and 306 of this Bibliography.

578. Spratt, P.F. "When Homer Nods." Letter to the editor. Ottawa Evening Citizen, 11 Oct. 1938, editorial page.

This letter objects to the phrase equally as in CE. (A debate followed. It consisted of letters to the press by J.H. Ogden "'When Homer Nods,'" Ottawa Citizen, 15 Oct. 1938; "Is It a Slovenly Expression?" ibid., 21 Oct. 1938; P.F. Spratt "More on 'Equally As,'" ibid., 25 Oct. 1938; J.H. Ogden "'Equally As'--a Rejoinder," ibid., 1 Nov. 1938; P.F. Spratt "The Last Word," E.A. Reynolds, "Equally With the Last Word," and F.J. MacNamara "Toronto Writer Equally Culpable," q.v., all ibid., 3 Nov. 1938.)

579. Stainsby, Donald. Review of A Dictionary of Canadianisms on Historical Principles, Walter S. Avis, Ed.-in-Chief. Vancouver Life, 17:1 (Sept. 1968), 13 and 15.

After a paragraph of Canadianisms, this review demonstrates how DCHP remedies the shortcomings of other dictionaries, and exemplifies its geographical range, its covering of sports, and its historical and political references.

580. Stewart, Loran. "Distinctive Canadian Dictionary Goal of RMC's Dr. Avis, Linguistic Expert." Kingston Whig-Standard, 20 Mar. 1957, p. 22.

This report of an interview with Walter S. Avis gives his view that CE is one of the definers of the Canadian national identity. There are many semantic Canadianisms, and 22 such are quoted, as well as 2 peculiarly Canadian pronunciations. CE also contains regionalisms, of which 4 are cited. Hence, a Canadian dictionary is needed, and the article describes the then state of the DCE project.

581. Stewart, William. "Friendly Plane Bomb You? Must Be 'Mitchellschmitt.'" Toronto Daily Star, 16 Feb. 1944, p. 3.

This article records 18 slang words and phrases, some of Italian origin, common in the speech of Canadian troops in Italy.

582. Stobie, Margaret. "A Bluff Is a Grove of Trees." ELN, 5 (1967), 49-51.

This article notes the Canadian meaning of bluff "grove of trees" and comments on its absence from DAE and DA. The origin of the meaning is attributed to synecdoche, and its history is traced from its Canadian beginning by quotations from The Nor'-Wester and The Manitoban newspapers.

583. Stoecker, Karin. "Canadian English Now Being Taught at University of N.B." Daily Gleaner (Fredericton N.B.), 4 Mar. 1972, p. 11.

This article records the view that there are several dialects in New Brunswick and exemplifies 1 lexical, 1 idiomatic, and 1 phonological feature from that area, along with an idiom from Newfoundland.

584. Story, G.M. "A Critical History of Dialect Collecting in Newfoundland." *RLS*, No. 6 (2 May 1975), p. 1-4.

This article names 26 persons who, from 1583 onwards, have commented on Newfoundland English. It adds some background information and evaluatory notes on 4 of them.

585. __________. "Dialect and the Standard Language." *Federation of Canadian Music Festivals Digest Report 1961*. n.p., n.d. p. 33-37.

This article is a slightly fuller version of that described in "Dialect Colors Newfoundland Speech," Anon., q.v.

586. __________. "Dialect and the Standard Language." *Journal of the Newfoundland Teachers' Association*, 49 (1957), 16-20.

This article is a slightly fuller version of that described in "Dialect Colors Newfoundland Speech," Anon., q.v.

587. __________. "The Dialects of Newfoundland." *Canadian Antiques Collector*, 10:2 (Mar.-Apr. 1975), 22-23.

The speech of Newfoundland reflects that province's Irish and West Country settlement, as also its later history. Its traditionalism is evidenced by 20 lexical, 1 morphological, 2 syntactical, and 8 phonological items. Its creativity is evidenced by 1 phonological item and 15 lexical items. The relationship between the speech of modern Newfoundland and its geography and culture is also discussed.

588. __________. "The Dialects of Newfoundland," in *The Book of Newfoundland*. Ed. Joseph R. Smallwood. St. John's, Nfld.: Newfoundland Book Publishers, 1967. Vol. III. 559-63.

This article shows how Newfoundland speech reflects the province's history and culture, giving 3 lexical examples of its conservatism and 5 of words evidenced from Newfoundland sources earlier than those cited in *OED*. Newfoundland speech is allied to Irish English by 9 lexical, 6 idiomatic, 2 phonological examples and 1 phonological feature, while 9 lexical, 6 morphological, 2 phonological examples and 2 phonological features ally it to West Country English. Its creativity is shown by 35 lexical examples. The article observes that

Story, G.M. Cont'd.

the dialects are resisting modern influences, while a general Newfoundland speech is emerging. Various examples are given of early observations and contemporary researches, and there is a bibliography of 26 items.

589. ________. "Newfoundland Dialect," in The Story of Newfoundland. Ed. A.B. Perlin. St. John's, Nfld.: n.p., 1959. p. 68-70.

This article points out that, as a result of Newfoundland's history and geography, its dialect shows both survival and innovation. The author cites 12 lexical, 6 phonological, and 6 morphological items connecting Newfoundland speech with that of the English West Country and 5 lexical items connecting it with Irish English. Newfoundland's linguistic inventiveness is illustrated by 33 lexical items and by 9 idioms. The current tendency towards a standard speech is discussed, and there is a bibliography of 9 items.

590. ________. "Newfoundland Dialect: An Historical View." Canadian Geographical Journal, 70 (1965), 126-31. Reprinted in Canadian English: Origins and Structures. Ed. J.K. Chambers (q.v.). p. 19-24.

After giving 6 lexical examples showing marine influence on Newfoundland dialect, this article surveys 8 writings mentioning Newfoundland speech. It cites 14 examples from these and notes that 1 article includes a glossary of about 200 words, 2 mention Newfoundland's dialectal diversity, and 2 others and, incidentally, the CBC wrongly connect Newfoundland speech with Irish English.

591. ________. A Newfoundland Dialect Dictionary: A Survey of the Problems. St. John's, Nfld.: Memorial Univ. of Newfoundland, 1956.

The author defines the scope of a dialect dictionary by listing the kinds of words it should include. The entry-selector's dilemma is shown by 1 example, while 3 show easier decisions. A further 63 examples show the richness of the Newfoundland vocabulary, while 12 show Newfoundland coinages. Phonological problems and their solutions are illustrated by 9 examples, etymological by 15, and semantic by 5. A final 5 examples illustrate the value of printed sources.

Story, G.M. Cont'd

592. __________. "Newfoundland and English Usage." Encyclopedia Canadiana, vol. 7 (Toronto: Grolier of Canada, 1957), 321-22.

After noting the variety of Newfoundland dialects, accountable to the province's history and geography, the author illustrates their outstanding features. In vocabulary, he cites 11 dialect survivals, 13 coinages, and 9 extensions of meaning. The alliance of lexical ingenuity with local activity is shown by 14 fishing, 3 sealing, and 2 logging terms, and by 10 terms for familiar surroundings. Features of sound and syntax were not then well enough known for description. The author concludes that a standard CE is a fiction.

593. __________. "Notes from a Berry Patch." PTRSC, 4th Series, Vol. 10 (1972), Sec II. p. 163-77.

As an appendix, this article contains a 700-word Newfoundland folk-tale, using quasi-phonetic spelling for some words.

594. __________. "Research in the Language and Place Names of Newfoundland." JCLA, 3 (1957), 47-55.

After dealing with place names, the author mentions the conditioning of Newfoundland speech by the island's history and geography. Its vocabulary shows survivals (9 examples), changes (3 examples), and inventions (9 examples). It is colourful (7 examples) and closely culture-related (7 examples). Plans for future studies of the language are described. A footnote gives 5 of its phonological and 6 of its morpho-syntactical features.

595. __________, and William J. Kirwin. "'The Dictionary of Newfoundland English': Progress and Promise." RLS, No. 5 (21 Jan. 1974), p. 15-17.

This article describes the development of the Dictionary of Newfoundland English. It will consist of words which are first recorded in Newfoundland or in books about Newfoundland, or which are otherwise considered to be Newfoundlandisms. The current state of the project is outlined, and the plans for its continuation are described.

Story, G.M., and William J. Kirwin. Cont'd.

596. [__________, and __________.] "Linguistic Atlas of Newfoundland Dialect Questionnaire." Mimeographed. St. John's, Nfld.: Memorial Univ. of Newfoundland, 1963.

This questionnaire has 400 items, keyed to the questionnaire of the LAUSC project. Some items demand more than one response from the informant. There is an index to lexical terms and selected topics.

597. __________, and __________. "National Dictionaries and Regional Homework." RLS, No. 3 (15 Jan. 1971), p. 19-22.

After outlining the history and methodology of DCHP, this article claims that its treatment of Newfoundland dialect is inadequate. Citing 22 entries which they regard as unsatisfactory for various reasons, the authors take the editors of DCHP to task for relying only on printed sources.

598. [__________, and __________.] "A Newfoundland Dialect Questionnaire: Avalon Peninsula. 1. Vocabulary." Mimeographed. St. John's, Nfld.: Memorial Univ. of Newfoundland, 1959.

This experimental questionnaire offers 306 Newfoundland linguistic forms grouped in batches of alternatives round 70 definitions.

599. __________, __________, and J.D.A. Widdowson. "Collecting for the Dictionary of Newfoundland English," in Lexicography in English. Ed. Raven I. McDavid, Jr. and Audrey Duckert (q.v.). p. 104-08.

After giving the criteria for the inclusion of a word, this article first characterizes the printed sources of such words. Oral sources are then classified: they consist of direct interviews, the products of focussed questionnaires, collections by folklore students, manuscript collections, the tape collection, investigations by student dialectologists, and contributions by individuals. The processing of each type of source is described.

Story, G.M., William J. Kirwin, and J.D.A. Widdowson. Cont'd.

600. [__________, __________, and __________.] "Selected Sample Entries." RLS, No. 6 (2 May 1975), p. 10-17.

The 23 sample entries, from Labrador marten to lun, illustrate the content of "Selecting and Presenting the Lexicon [in the Dictionary of Newfoundland English]" by William J. Kirwin, q.v.

601. Strong, William Duncan. "More Labrador Survivals." AS, 6 (1931), 290-91.

This article is based on observations made by the author during a 15-month stay in Labrador in 1927-1928. It cites 20 general vocabulary items, 6 pronoun usages, 1 verbal idiom, 1 item of pronunciation, and 6 sea-related terms, all characteristic of Labrador speech.

602. Stuck, Walter. "Dictionary of Canadian English." NS, 68=N.S. 18 (1969), 306-10.

This article prefaces reviews of BD, ID, SD, and DCHP with a 4-paragraph quotation from SD, illustrating the individuality of CE, and with a comment on the excellence of the idea of grading the dictionaries. It lists 9 characteristics for BD, 7 for ID, and 12 for SD and quotes a specimen entry from each. For DCHP, it summarizes that dictionary's history of CE, giving 12 examples of the results thereof. Finally, it quotes approvingly DCHP's doctrine on CE and gives a specimen of the dictionary's entries.

603. __________. "Dictionary of Canadian English." Die Realschule (Verband Deutschen Realschullehrer, München), No. 4 (Apr. 1969), p. 15-16.

This is a briefer version of the same author's article in NS under the same title, q.v.

604. __________. "Dominion: Eine kurze Untersuchung zur Gültigkeit des Begriffes." NS, 69=N.S. 19 (1970), 611-19.

This article traces the use of the word dominion in and as applied to Canada. It is gradually being replaced by federal and by Canada. The DCHP entries including dominion are quoted, and the names of a number of organizations that use the word are given.

605. Svartengren, T. Hilding. "The Feminine Gender for Inanimate Things in Anglo-American." *AS*, 3 (1927-1928), 83-113.

Scattered through this article are several instances of the use by various Canadian writers of feminine-gender pronouns referring to inanimate objects.

606. Swift, W.H. "'Whom' is a Dodo or The Bell Tolls for 'Whom.'" *Canadian Education*, 12:3 (June 1957), 38-43.

This article notes that *who* is increasingly replacing *whom* in sentence-initial position in CE.

607. Syford, Constance Miriam. "'Burn-out.'" *AS*, 16 (1941), 315-16.

This article claims that novelist Wallace Stegner's use of *burn-out* refers to land laid waste by fire and is a Canadianism.

608. Szwed, John Francis. *Private Cultures and Public Imagery: Interpersonal Relations in a Newfoundland Peasant Society*. Newfoundland Social and Economic Studies, 2. St. John's, Nfld.: Memorial Univ. of Newfoundland, 1966.

A number of words and idioms from the speech of this community in southwest Newfoundland are cited and explained *passim* in this work.

609. Taylor, James. *Narrative of a Voyage to, and Travels in Upper Canada, with Accounts of the Customs, Character, and Dialect of the Country, Also Remarks on Emigration, Agriculture, Etc*. Hull (England): John Nicholson, 1846.

The section on customs, character, and dialect of the country (p. 45-51) reports on 6 idioms then current in CE, as well as commenting on the nasality and on the "majestic manner" of the utterance of Canadians. Females are said to have melodious voices.

610. Thomas, Charles Kenneth. *An Introduction to the Phonetics of American English*. 2nd ed. New York: Ronald, 1958.

Comments on 6 features of Canadian pronunciation appear on

p. 51, 117, 119, 141, 144, 173, 210, 211, 230, and 231 of this work. The uselessness in Canada of An English Pronouncing Dictionary by Daniel Jones, 11th ed. (New York: E.P. Dutton, 1956), is noted on p. 258.

611. Thompson, Thomas C. "Chimo." Letter to the editor. Globe and Mail (Toronto), 1 May 1969, p. 6.

The writer notes that, during his stay at Fort Chimo, the name was pronounced, both there and at Royal Canadian Air Force headquarters in Ottawa, with its accented vowel riming with sky.

612. Tomkinson, Grace. "Shakespeare in Newfoundland." DR, 20 (1940), 60-70.

Along with comment on the dialectal diversity and on other aspects of Newfoundland culture, the author records 2 morphological features, with 3 examples of each, from Newfoundland speech. She also records 160 lexical items, characterizing 66 as localisms, 19 as archaisms, and 38 as survivals from Elizabethan and earlier times. A further 4 are of West Country origin, 2 are Newfoundland coinages, 26 originate in languages or dialects not current in England, and 5 are of unknown etymology.

613. Trent, Bill. "They Have A Word For It." Weekend Magazine, 13 May 1961, p. 28-29.

Anticipating the appearance of the first dictionary in the DCE series, this article gives a brief account of the origin of DCE, with biographical references to 4 of its editors, and cites 17 examples of regional variation in the vocabulary of CE.

614. Trueblood, Thomas C. "Spoken English." QJS, 19 (1933), 513-21.

According to this article, the author had observed practically no difference between the English spoken south of the Canada-United States border from Montreal to Vancouver and that spoken north of it.

615. Tuttle, Florence W. "Better Overhaul Your Slang, It Reveals More Than You Know." SatN, 15 Jan. 1944, p. 18.

This article points out that slang words and phrases perish and that their continued use after their demise "dates" the user; 25 such dead phrases are quoted. The author then quotes 13 further expressions from services slang to illustrate slang then still fresh.

616. [Tweedie, W.M., and Rev. William Pilot.] "New Brunswick, Nova Scotia, and Newfoundland." DN, 1 (1890-1896), 377-81. [This item was ed. E.H. Babbitt and others.]

This lists 129 words in all. Of these, 3 are attributed to Nova Scotia and 17 to Newfoundland, 1 is said to be common to New Brunswick and Nova Scotia, and 1 to New Brunswick and Newfoundland. Quotations, more or less illustrative, accompany 13 of the words.

617. Urion, Carl. "Canadian English and Canadian French (a review)," in Linguistic Diversity in Canadian Society. Ed. Regna Darnell (q.v.). p. 33-44.

This article reviews Speaking Canadian English and Speaking Canadian French, both by Mark M. Orkin, q.v. The reviewer notes that Orkin's work is informal and that its main value lies in the questions it raises. He lists the contents of Speaking Canadian English and assesses its treatment of loanwords, of the relationship of the English and French languages, and of the history, dialects, phonology, syntax, and etymology of CE.

618. ________. "A German-English Interlingual 'Key,'" in Linguistic Diversity in Canadian Society. Ed. Regna Darnell (q.v.). p. 223-30.

Based on a study of an English-German bilingual family in Alberta, this article notes three kinds of use of German in English speech. Conclusions are drawn regarding who uses German most and to whom it is most used. The author gives 7 lexical, 3 phonological, and 2 morphological examples with their sociological contexts, and the social purposes of the use of German are outlined.

619. Vinay, J.-P., Walter S. Avis, G. Dulong, D.M. Grubb, J. Poirier, and J.B. Rudnyckyj. "Linguistica Canadiana: A Linguistic Bibliography for 1968 and Supplement for Previous Years." CJL, 15 (1969), 51-81.

This bibliography lists 6 books (including 1 bibliography, 3 dictionaries, and 1 glossary), 47 articles (including 1 bibliography), 1 pamphlet, and 2 theses, all devoted entirely to CE or to the investigation thereof. It lists also 3 books which give considerable space to the study of CE.

620. __________, and Pierre Daviault. "Dictionnaires Canadiens: I, Les Dictionnaires Bilingues." Journal des Traducteurs-Translators' Journal, 3 (1958), 109-13.

This article gives the purpose of the then proposed bilingual dictionary: it is to enshrine the Canadianism of both Canadian French and CE, and to increase the general understanding of texts in both languages. The lexicographers' methods and criteria are described, and there is an account of the staffing and operation of the Centre de Recherches lexicographiques. The prior appearance of DCCD is forecast.

621. __________, __________, and Henry Alexander. Dictionnaire Canadien/The Canadian Dictionary. Concise Edition. Toronto: McClelland and Stewart, 1962.

The front matter in this bilingual work includes a preface which states the dictionary's aim and a note on the English spelling which discusses 6 spelling features, the spelling of 15 words, and the treatment of compounds. A note sur la transcription phonetique de l'Anglo-Canadien explains that the transcription is mainly francophone-oriented. A note sur la phonologie de l'Anglo-Canadien gives the dictionary's authorities for pronunciation. This note then points out that the pronunciation of CE is a mixture of BE and AE, with some Canadianisms, but that this pronunciation shows a surprising homogeneity; the note then discusses and exemplifies 10 phonological features of CE. There is a tableau des symboles phonetiques anglais. The English section of the dictionary contains an estimated 11,000 entries, including a number of regionalisms.

622. W., J. "That Fourth Syllable." Letter to the editor. Ottawa Evening Journal, 13 Dec. 1939, p. 6.

This notes the use of "'mayorality' in four syllables" for mayoralty.

623. Walker, Douglas C. "Another Edmonton Idiolect: Comments on an Article by Professor Avis," in Canadian English: Origins and Structures. Ed. J.K. Chambers (q.v.). p. 129-32.

The author compares several Edmonton idiolects, including his own, with that reported in "The Phonemic Segments of an Edmonton Idiolect" by Walter S. Avis, q.v. He differs from or extends Avis's views about 6 vocalic features (giving 31 examples in all) and about 3 consonantal features (giving 11 examples in all). He transcribes phonetically 15 words quoted by Avis and suggests further lines of research.

624. Walker, Laurence. "Dialect and Reading in Newfoundland Schools." Morning Watch, 2:2 (Jan. 1975), 3-6.

In handling the problems which non-standard dialect poses for the teacher of English, the author gives 1 example of each of 11 phonological features of Newfoundland dialect and 5 examples of a twelfth feature. He implies the existence of 4 morphological variations, giving 1, 2, 3, and 6 examples, respectively. There are also 4 examples of dialect items in the lexicon.

625. _________. Newfoundland Dialect Interference in Oral Reading. ERIC Document Reproduction Service, ED 092 900, CS 001 173. Washington, D.C.: U.S. Department of Health, Education and Welfare, 1974. Reprinted in Journal of Reading Behaviour, 7:1 (Spring 1975), 61-78.

This study includes (p. 9-12) a description and exemplification of 8 morphological features from the dialects of Grand Bank and of Carbonear, Nfld. It also briefly discusses the similarity of these to the features of Black English.

626. _________, and Harold [J.] Paddock. "Spelling and the Newfoundland Dialect." Morning Watch, 2:4 (May 1975), 9-13.

This article lists 2 morphological and 12 phonological features of Newfoundland dialect and gives from 1 to 6 examples of each, showing how each may produce a particular spelling error. It also lists 2 lexical items from Newfoundland dialect whose pronunciation may likewise have produced spelling errors.

Walker, Laurence, and Harold [J.] Paddock. Cont'd.

627. __________, __________, Lloyd Brown, and Ishmael Baksh. "Nonstandard Dialect and Literacy: An In-service Project in Newfoundland." Interchange, 6:3 (1975), 4-10.

As part of its background information, this article mentions 3 features of Newfoundland speech, giving 2 examples of each of the first 2, and 1 of the third. It also exemplifies 1 feature of Newfoundland morphology.

628. Wanamaker, M[urray] G[orham]. "Canadian English: Whence? Whither?" Journal of Education (Nova Scotia), 9 (1959), 22-26.

This article argues the case for the then embryonic DCE, and outlines the project and its method. It also gives specific information for those who may be interested in reading for the project.

629. __________. "The Language of Kings County, Nova Scotia." Ph.D. thesis. Univ. of Michigan, 1965. See Dissertation Abstracts, 26 (1965), 2740-41.

The introduction explains that this thesis is based on 21 field records made with the LAUSC Short Work Sheets, and it also gives a list of all 71 field records made in Nova Scotia to its date. The linguistic chapters deal with 59 characteristic features of vocabulary, with 24 verbal and 12 non-verbal morphological features, and with 15 stressed and 2 unstressed vocalics, giving also a note on some consonantals. The last chapter draws general conclusions. Appended matter includes a description of the informants and their communities, a bibliography, and an index of features cited. There are 81 figures in the text.

630. __________. "Nips, Chips, and Holy Water." PLCMND, 13 (1973), 13-15.

After illustrating regional variety in CE, the author shows the difficulty of collecting phonological information through a postal questionnaire, and of presenting phonological information in a dictionary. There is a brief comparison of the systems used to indicate pronunciation in 3 Canadian and 4 American dictionaries, and the importance of some knowledge of the International Phonetic Alphabet is stressed.

Wanamaker, M[urray] G[orham]. Cont'd.

631. _________. "Survey of Canadian English--Focus on Manitoba." Classmate (Official Publication of the Manitoba Association of Teachers of English), 4:2 (Winter 1974), 37-43.

After outlining some of the difficulties involved in using a written questionnaire, the author mentions, with reservations, the possibility that there are 2 dialects of English in Manitoba. He then gives a carefully detailed account of a student-run Survey of Manitoba English and contrasts some of its results with those of the SCE.

632. _________. "Your Dialect Is Showing," in Looking at Language. Ed. M.H. Scargill and P.G. Penner (q.v.). p. 104-13.

After defining a dialect, the author gives the sources of CE and characterizes CE as being itself a dialect. But CE also contains dialects, as is shown by 4 lexical examples. The reader is invited to measure CE by comparing it with 24 spellings, 6 pronunciations, and 10 lexical items. There is a short list of works containing CE dialect.

633. Ward, Norman. "Talk Canadian!" Quarterly of Canadian Studies, 1 (1972), 164-67.

This article objects to the misuse in Canadian political writings of term, prime minister elect, appointment of Speaker, and elected office (sc. of the premiership).

634. _________. "Talk Canadian!" Reader's Digest, Sept. 1972, p. 8.

This is a digest of "Talk Canadian!" by the same author, in the Quarterly of Canadian Studies, q.v.

635. Warkentyne, H.J. "Contemporary Canadian English." [1973]. AS, 46 (1971), 193-99.

This article first traces the history of the SCE, and briefly discusses its questionnaire. It then describes the results. The existence of a generation gap is shown by 19 examples. In regional variation, Newfoundland, the East, and the West are set off from each other by 11 features, British Columbia being further separated by 2 more. The effects of education on usage are shown by a further 38 examples.

636. Weber, Debby. "Canadian Raising in a Windsor, Ontario, Dialect." CWPL, 1:1 (1975), 22-25.

Based on 40 examples, this article modifies the rule stated in "Canadian Raising" by J.K. Chambers, q.v., to explain the wider domain in the idiolect examined of [ʌy] and [ʌw].

637. Weber, W.G. "Up the Crick." Reader's Digest, Sept. 1972, p. 57.

This article notes the pronunciation of creek with /ɪ/, apparently from British Columbia.

638. Welch, Kay. "Australian Lowering: A Study of One Dialect Difference Between Canadian and Australian Spoken English." CWPL, 1:1 (1975), 44-46.

Comparing her own Australian idiolect with evidence from classroom pronunciation of 17 selected words from CE, the author concludes that there is a lowering rule for /i/ before /r/ in Australian English but not in CE.

639. West, Michael, and William F. Mackey. Canadian Reader's Dictionary. Don Mills, Ont.: Longmans Canada, and Montreal: Centre Educatif et Culturel, 1968.

This dictionary contains over 24,000 main entries, including 300 Canadian terms and a number of words with special Canadian meanings. Its introduction draws attention to the variations in Canadian pronunciation, giving 8 examples of words whose pronunciation varies thus. The dictionary itself, however, records only 1 pronunciation for each word.

640. White, Jack A. "The Newfoundland Word Man." Atlantic Advocate, 48:4 (Dec. 1957), 40-44.

This article reports as G.M. Story's the views which follow. The dialectal diversity of the original settlers, combined with geographical isolation, gives Newfoundland its present speech; but Newfoundlanders possess linguistic ingenuity (2 examples) and a unique dialect (1 example). The article gives 1 example for each of the 6 parts of the planned Newfoundland dictionary. Finally, Newfoundland dialect is exemplified by 16 words from sealing, 23 from fishing, 7 from food, by 3 fish names, and by 6 topological words.

641. Widdowson, J.D.A. "The Dialect of Fortune Harbour, Newfoundland: A Pronouncing Glossary." FoLi, 2 (1968), 316-26.

This article is based on visits to almost every house in the chosen community and on 14 extensive interviews and 6 extensive tape recordings. The glossary gives 481 items, most with distinctively Newfoundland pronunciations or senses. They are classified as marine (121), lumbering (51), agricultural (38), and general (271). Phonetic script is used to indicate the pronunciation(s) of each word, and 147 of the words are defined.

642. ________. "Mummering and Janneying: Some Explanatory Notes," in Christmas Mumming in Newfoundland: Essays in Anthropology, Folklore and History. Ed. H. Halpert and G.M. Story. Toronto: Univ. of Toronto for Memorial Univ. of Newfoundland, 1969. p. 216-21.

The author notes that on the east and south coasts of Newfoundland the usual terms for disguised Christmas house-visitors and their activities are mummers and mummering, respectively. On the west coast, the terms are janney and janneying. Where both sets co-exist, the former is usually regarded as the older. Janney is probably derived from a West of England pronunciation of Johnny 'a bumpkin.' Finally, the article records 5 other Newfoundland words for mummers.

643. ________. "Settlement Patterns and Newfoundland Folklore." The Graduate Society of Memorial University of Newfoundland, 1967. Ed. D.H. Barnes and R.J. Wiseman. St. John's, Nfld.: Memorial Univ. of Newfoundland, 1967. p. 14-15.

This summary of the author's thesis points out that the settlement pattern of Newfoundland is the basis for the patterns of speech, richly diverse though now somewhat blurred, which exist in Newfoundland.

644. ________. "Some Items of a Central Newfoundland Dialect." CJL, 10 (1964), 37-46.

This article is based on field interviews with 16 informants, most from Bishop's Falls, Nfld. Under 4 arbitrary headings, the author transcribes phonetically 179 words or phrases and notes 1 morphological feature and 7 phonological features, including 1 which differentiates speech of English origin from that of Irish origin. Under a fifth heading, he gives

Widdowson, J.D.A. Cont'd.

1 phonological feature, with 8 examples, and 12 morphological features, including 1 differentiating feature, with 4 examples. He also notes and exemplifies 8 syntactical features and 1 lexical feature. He ends by suggesting examination of the newer communities wherein the English-based and Irish-based Newfoundland dialects may be merging.

645. ________. "A Survey of Current Folklore Research in Newfoundland, with special reference to the English West Country." Transactions of the Devonshire Association, 101 (1969), 183-96.

Noting that English in Newfoundland reflects the province's settlement pattern, the article gives 21 examples of words or phrases peculiar to, or with meanings peculiar to, Newfoundland. A further 51 lexical examples relate the English of Newfoundland to that of the West Country; so, too, does 1 phonological feature, of which 17 examples are given, and so, too, do 3 morphological features. The author cites 3 other lexical items from Newfoundland child lore, 13 from custom and belief, and 1 from folk drama.

646. Wightman, F.A. "Maritime Provincialisms and Contrasts: Words, Phrases and Expressions." Canadian Magazine, 39 (May-Oct. 1912), 3-7.

This article mentions 6 pronunciations limited to the Maritimes and of New England origin, and 1 limited to Nova Scotia and of German origin. It discusses 7 words with meanings peculiar to Prince Edward Island and speculates as to their origins. It mentions 1 word which that province shares with New Brunswick and lists 2 words peculiar to western New Brunswick. The word var is said to be in general Maritime use, and the use of whatever for emphasis in Prince Edward Island and in Cape Breton Island is also noted and illustrated.

647. Williams, Joseph M. Origins of the English Language: A Social and Linguistic History. New York: Free Press, 1975. p. 276.

This argues that the durative be in Eastern Canada and Newfoundland is inherited from the Southern dialect of (nonstandard) BE, not copied from Black English.

648. Williamson, Juanita V., and Virginia M. Burke. A Various Language: Perspectives on American Dialects. New York: Holt, Rinehart and Winston, 1971.

This anthology contains items 126 and 444 of this Bibliography.

649. Willis, Clodius. The Development of an Automatic Dialect Classification Test: Final Report. ERIC Document Reproduction Service, ED 041 263, AL 002 464. Washington, D.C.: U.S. Department of Health, Education and Welfare, 1969.

Although not primarily concerned with CE, the author notes that, compared to speakers of the Buffalo Dialect of AE, speakers of the Fort Erie, Ont., dialect of CE distinguish more easily between /ɛ/ and /æ/, probably have a more retracted boundary between /æ/ and /ɑ/, and probably have higher boundaries between /i/ and /e/ and between /o/ and /u/. He correlates the first of these results with the phonic difference between /æ/ in Fort Erie speech and /æ/ in Buffalo speech. He correlates the second with the CE homophony of cot and caught, and the third with a hypothetical CE monophthongal pronunciation of /e/ and /o/.

650. __________. "Individual and Dialectal Variation in the Perception of Synthetic Vowels." Ph.D. thesis. Univ. of Rochester, 1970. See DAI A, 31 (1970), 1787A-88A.

The summary of this thesis in DAI is identical with the summary preceding The Development of An Automatic Dialect Classification Test: Final Report by this author, q.v.

651. __________. "Perception of Vowel Phonemes in Fort Erie Ontario, Canada, and Buffalo, New York: An Application of Synthetic Vowel Categorization Tests to Dialectology." JSHR, 15 (1972), 246-55.

This is a more condensed presentation of some of the material in The Development of an Automatic Dialect Classification Test: Final Report by this author, q.v.

652. __________. "Synthetic Vowel Categorization and Dialectology." L&S, 14 (1971), 213-28.

This is a more condensed presentation of some of the material in The Development of an Automatic Dialect Classification Test: Final Report by this author, q.v.

653. Wilson, Eric. "Dictionary of Canadianism." _Ottawa Journal_, 26 Mar. 1966, p. [34].

This article on the then forthcoming _DCHP_ mentions its size and outlines its history. It exemplifies 6 Canadianisms from the field of nicknames and lists 8 more, of which it illustrates 1 by quotation.

654. Wilson, Harold. "'Crosshanded' and 'Sad.'" _AS_, 13 (1938), 236.

This article gives the special Newfoundland meaning of the first and the special New Brunswick meaning of the second of the words in its title. It adds a note on the history of each.

655. Wilson, H[arry] Rex. "Canadian English," in _The Doubleday Dictionary for Home, School, and Office_. Ed. Sidney I. Landau and Ronald J. Bogus. New York: Doubleday, 1975. p. xxv-xxvii.

Under origins, the writer notes that CE's realization of /r/ justifies the popular opinion that CE resembles AE more than it resembles BE. Under pronunciation, he describes 1 distinctive feature and 5 specific words, 2 showing BE influence, and he also mentions the general homogeneity of CE outside the Atlantic Provinces. Under spelling, the survival of BE influence, thanks to Canadian immunity from Websterian reforms, is remarked and thrice exemplified. Under vocabulary, 26 Canadianisms are listed, including 8 coinages, and 2, 4, 2, and 10 terms are drawn from sport, administrative history, technology, and linguistic borrowing, respectively.

656. ________. "Dialect, An Informal Record of History." _Transactions of the Illinois State Academy of Science_, 44 (1951), 190-95.

While mainly concerned with dialects in AE, this article mentions that in one Nova Scotia village the distinctive dialect is probably the best clue to the provenance of the original settlers. In another, the dialect derived from the speech of the original settlers is still the "prestige" form. The circulation of _shivaree_ in the St. Lawrence Valley and the rivalry of _coal oil_ and _kerosene_ in Ontario are also indices of cultural history.

Wilson, H[arry] Rex. Cont'd.

657. __________. "Dialect literature: A two-way street?" CJL, 18 (1973), 157-62.

Although mainly concerned with theory, this article notes that Haliburton's Sam Slick writings accurately represent the /r/-less speech current in the Annapolis Valley and the South Shore of Nova Scotia in the early nineteenth century.

658. __________. "The Dialect of Lunenburg County, Nova Scotia." Ph.D. thesis. Univ. of Michigan, 1958. See Dissertation Abstracts, 19 (1959), 3300-01.

The first two chapters of this thesis deal with its methods and with the cultural background of the area studied. Then, under vocabulary, influences from AE are noted and contrasts within the area are described. Under morphology, verb forms, undeclined phrases, and pronouns are discussed. In phonology, 18 features of the speech of the area are detailed. The last chapter gives general conclusions. A bibliography is included.

659. __________. "It's broader than beer parlor and baby bonus." Globe Magazine, 8 Apr. 1967, p. 19.

This review of SD gives that dictionary's place in the DCE series and relates SD to the work of Thorndike and Barnhart. The review then mentions SD's selection of words, giving 3 examples, and glances, with 1 example, at SD's treatment of spelling. SD's treatment of pronunciation (4 examples), its usage notes, its illustrations, and its quotations (1 example) are also mentioned, as are its typography and the displaying of its pronunciation guide.

660. __________. "Lunenburg Dutch: Fact and Folklore," in Canadian English: Origins and Structures. Ed. J.K. Chambers (q.v.). p. 40-44.

This is a 5-page summary of "The Dialect of Lunenburg County, Nova Scotia" by **this author, q.v.**

661. __________. Report of the Canadian Regional Secretary of the American Dialect Society. NADS, 5:1 (Feb. 1973), 26.

This report outlines work then in progress on CE.

Wilson, H[arry] Rex. Cont'd.

662. ________. Report of the Canadian Regional Secretary of the American Dialect Society. NADS, 7:1 and 2 (Feb., June 1975), 14-15.

This report outlines work then in progress on CE.

663. Wilson, Leslie. "Canada's First Dictionary Said Businessman's Helper." Financial Post, 13 Apr. 1957. p. 1.

This description of the then forthcoming DCCD names its editors and indicates the 3 main linguistic functions it will perform. Its usefulness to the businessman is also forecast and 2 illustrations of this are given.

664. The Winston Canadian Dictionary for School, Home, and Office. Toronto: Holt, Rinehart and Winston of Canada, [1973].

This is The Winston Canadian Dictionary for Schools, q.v., with a slightly revised foreword.

665. The Winston Canadian Dictionary for Schools. Toronto: Holt, Rinehart and Winston of Canada, [1960], 1965.

This dictionary contains about 38,000 entries. However, few are Canadianisms, and those which are, are not so marked.

666. Wintemberg, W.J. "Hickory." JAF, 16 (1903), 128.

This notes the use by German residents of Waterloo County, Ont., of the word hickory for a "Pennsylvania Dutchman."

667. ________. "'Squaw Winter,' 'Indian Winter,' 'Dogwood Winter.'" JAF, 20 (1907), 235-36.

This article notes the use of the term squaw winter in the Toronto Daily Star of 8 Apr. 1907, and the use of Indian winter in conversation in Toronto on 15 Apr. 1904. Both terms refer to a snowfall in April.

668. Woods, Howard Bruce. "A Case for the Danish Element in Northern American." M.A. thesis. Univ. of British Columbia, 1969.

This thesis notes (p. 104) that the office of ombudsman, and hence probably the word, first appeared in North America in the province of Alberta. It also quotes (p. 105 and 106) 8 food-related words of Scandinavian origin current in Vancouver.

669. Young, Audrey, and Evelyn Pearce. An editorial. _Canadian Council of Teachers of English Newsletter_, 7:1 (Sept. 1973), n. pag.

This paragraph recounts a first comment by M.H. Scargill on the results of the SCE. Scargill noted a relationship between CE and some BE of Yorkshire and Cornwall.

670. Young, Scott. "It's Strictly Pusser." _Maclean's Magazine_, 15 Aug. 1943, p. 10 and 44-46.

This article records and defines 50 R.C.A.F., 21 R.C.N., and 7 Canadian army slang terms, as well as 3 slang terms common to all services. It speculates on the origin of 3 of the terms.

671. ________. "Slang Enriches Language." _Globe and Mail (Toronto)_, 7 Aug. 1957, p. 11.

This article records 3 examples of slang heard in radio sports broadcasts in Toronto and then lists 10 examples of Second World War slang which have fallen out of use and 13 which are still current. It ends with a punning, quasi-phonetic alphabet, lacking entries for _Q_, _S_, _W_, and _Y_.

ADDENDUM

672. Anon. "A local expression--You're right welcome." Valley Visitor (Woodstock, N.B.: Bugle Press), 5:1 (26 June-9 July 1976), 13. Reprinted in later issues of this same volume.

This article combines "Climbing fool's hill," "A local expression," and "Local figures of speech," all Anon., q.v.

*673. ________. "The Raconteur." Gazette (Montreal), 19 Jan. 1924, p. 37.

Mainly a review of an unspecified edition of The American Language by H.L. Mencken, this mentions the CE use of rabbit for 'hare,' quotes a correspondent's opinion that the speech of Toronto resembles that of Buffalo, N.Y., and speculates on the reason for the /l/ often heard in conflab.

674. Anon. (CP). "Mr. Goes Way of The Passenger Pigeon." Daily Gleaner (Fredericton, N.B.), 28 Feb. 1977, p. 2.

This records that the Canadian Press will no longer use the title Mr.

675. Avis, Walter S. "Canadian English," in Funk and Wagnalls Standard College Dictionary: Canadian Edition. Ed. Walter S. Avis, 1976 (q.v.). p. xv-xvi.

This is an updating of "Canadian English and Native Dictionaries" by Walter S. Avis, q.v.

*676. ________. "Dictionaries for Canadian English." Voxair (Canadian Forces Base, Winnipeg), 28 Feb. 1968, p. 3.

This is a condensed version of "Canadian English and Native Dictionaries" by Walter S. Avis, q.v.

Avis, Walter S. Cont'd.

*677. __________. "Some French-Canadian Loanwords in Canadian English." Signum (Royal Military College of Canada), 2:1 (Jan. 1975), 1-13.

An introduction shows the fate of 9 loanwords borrowed from French into CE. The article then selects 5 of these and 5 more and traces in detail, with illustrative quotations, their semantic and syntactic behaviour in CE. The information used is drawn from the files of DCHP.

678. __________. "We should use our dictionaries." Letter to the editor. Whig-Standard (Kingston, Ont.), 8 Mar. 1977, p. 7.

This is a rejoinder to the Editor's Note appended to "Faux Pas?" by Margaret Shortliffe, q.v. It cites 8 dictionaries which record a pejorative sense for henchman.

679. __________, ed. Funk and Wagnalls Standard College Dictionary: Canadian Edition. Toronto: Fitzhenry and Whiteside, 1976.

With the same front matter as the 1973 edition, q.v., this edition has a much increased Canadian content. It contains several hundred Canadian terms and definitions and includes, as end matter, 10 pages of Canadiana, such as the Canadian Bill of Rights, the list of the Fathers of Confederation, etc.

680. __________, R.J. Gregg, and M.H. Scargill, eds. The Canadian Junior Dictionary. Toronto: Gage Educational Publishing, 1977.

This is based on BD. With the same pronunciation key, it is otherwise a new edition, wholly revised, updated, and expanded.

681. Bähr, Dieter. "A Bibliography of Writings on the English Language in Canada: From 1857 to 1976." Anglistische Forschungen, 116. Heidelberg: Winter, 1977.

The first section of this work is a bibliography of 438 entries. As well as covering CE, it lists material on languages in contact, language shifts, and onomastics. The second section is a bibliographical guide to the study of CE, which classifies 412 of the entries in the bibliography under 7 main and 31 subordinate subject headings. Some of the entries appear under more than one heading.

682. Batten, Jack. "Toronto Speak." Globe and Mail (Toronto), 4 May 1977, p. 3.

This article claims, not altogether seriously, to recognize 4 Toronto dialects, varying in clarity of enunciation, volume range, syntax, and vocabulary.

*683. Carson, Jo. "Linguist hopes to save endangered dialects." Globe and Mail (Toronto), 13 Nov. 1975, p. F 10.

This report of an interview with J.K. Chambers describes his view that television is spreading an urban dialect and destroying local dialects. This urban dialect, derived originally from BE, has now no counterpart therein. Fashion, style, political leadership, etc. are mentioned as influencing language. The need for recording dialectal diversity before the dialects disappear is emphasized.

*684. Chambers, J.K. "Linguistics in the English classroom." EE, 8 (1966), 2-17.

The authors could not obtain a copy of this before going to press.

*685. ________. "A modest proposal for first-language teaching." EE, 15 (1973), 26-40.

The authors could not obtain a copy of this before going to press.

*686. ________. "Wonder of wonders: lucidity for non-parsing scribblers." Globe and Mail (Toronto), 9 Dec. 1972, p. 33.

This review of A Grammar of Contemporary English by Randolph Quirk et al. (New York: Seminar, 1972) notes that exclamations of the type Did he ever clobber the goalie! are common in CE and AE but are not mentioned in the work reviewed.

687. Colombo, John Robert. Colombo's Concise Canadian Quotations. Edmonton: Hurtig, 1976.

Quotations relating to CE appear on p. 17b, 79a, 102a, 109b, 121a, 121b (2), 163b, 197b, 203a, 203b, and 212a. Except for that on p. 197b, all appear also in Colombo's Canadian Quotations by the same author, q.v.

*688. Courtney, Maureen Rosemary. "Lexical Choice as an Index of Acculturation: Fifteen Case Studies." M.A. thesis. Univ. of Victoria, Victoria, B.C., 1972.

The responses of 4 women, native residents of Victoria, B.C., to a questionnaire of 491 items are recorded and discussed _passim_ in this study. The study also contains (p. 28-42) an essay, "British and Canadian English," based to some extent on work published in _JCLA_.

689. Davidson, J.A. "Say that again." _Globe and Mail_ (Toronto), 29 Apr. 1976, p. 47.

This article notes the obtrusiveness to American ears of CE /r/ and /aʊ/. It includes some quotation from the same author's "Our very own sounds," q.v.

690. Drysdale, P.D. Letter to the editor. _Verbatim_, 2:4 (Feb. 1976), 13.

Citing _DCHP_, the author adds _shebang_ and _shanty_ to a list of loans from Celtic into English. He also asks for more information on the lumbering sense of _to barber chair_.

*691. England, George Allan. "Glossary of Commonly Used Newfoundland Words and Phrases," in _The Greatest Hunt in the World_. Montreal: Tundra Books, 1969.

This is a reprint of the "Glossary of Commonly Used Newfoundland Words and Phrases" in _Vikings of the Ice_ by the same author, q.v.

692. Falk, Lilian. "On the attitudes to dialect differences in Canada." _SIFT_. Dept. of English, St. Mary's Univ., Halifax, N.S.

The authors could not obtain a copy of this before going to press.

693. Galloway, Priscilla. Review of _The Winston Dictionary of Canadian English_. Elementary Edition. Ed. Thomas M. Paikeday and others, and of _The Canadian Junior Dictionary_. Ed. Walter S. Avis and others. _EngQ_, 9:4 (Winter 1976/1977), 118-20.

This review compares these dictionaries with regard to range of entries, definitions, spelling, pronunciation guides, incidental information, illustrations, and format.

694. Garner, Hugh. "Quote and Digger Man." Books in Canada, 6:1 (Jan. 1977), 3-5.

This is a review of Colombo's Concise Canadian Quotations by John Robert Colombo, q.v., and of Colombo's Canadian References by John Robert Colombo (Toronto: O.U.P., 1976). It cites chesterfield 'couch,' concession 'road,' and pogey 'unemployment insurance' as Canadianisms.

695. Gibson, Deborah Jean. "A Thesis on Eh." M.A. thesis. Univ. of British Columbia, 1976.

The data used for this thesis consist of more than 550 occurrences of eh from 74 Vancouver informants. These occurrences were classified into 8 grammatical and stylistic types: Reversed Polarity; Constant Polarity; Imperative; Exclamation; Polar Interrogative; Wh-Question; Pardon; and Anecdotal. The last was the type most often used by the informants. Analysis indicates that eh is used mostly in informal speech.

696. Johnson, Marion R. "Canadian Eh." Ohio State Univ. Working Papers in Linguistics, 21 (1976), 153-160.

The authors could not obtain a copy of this before going to press.

697. Kalbfleisch, John. "Could You Say That in Canadian, Please?" Weekend Magazine, 16 Oct. 1976, p. 18 and 21.

This review of Funk and Wagnalls Standard College Dictionary: Canadian Edition, ed. Walter S. Avis, q.v., draws attention to the increased Canadianism thereof. It cites 88 lexical items from the dictionary as evidence of this. Pronunciation, spelling, and the general background of CE are all mentioned.

*698. Kenwood, Christopher Michael. "A Study of Slang and Informal Usage in the Newspaper." M.A. thesis. Univ. of British Columbia, 1969.

The main part of this thesis is a glossary of 780 slang words and phrases culled from the Vancouver Sun and the Vancouver Province. Each entry is accompanied by a phonemic transcription, a definition, and a source identification. Some are accompanied by other information as well.

699. Kerner, Fred. "A Word to the Wise." CAB, 51:3 (Spring 1976), 15.

This article comments disparagingly on the use in "the contemporary press" of transpire as 'happen.'

700. ________. "A Word to the Wise." CAB, 51:4 (Summer 1976), 15.

This article comments disapprovingly on the commonness in spoken CE of an excrescent /ə/ after the /l/ of elm and film and after the first syllable of fiscal and minster.

701. [Kirwin, William J., and Paddock, Harold J.] "Linguistic Research in Newfoundland." RLS, No. 7 (22 June 1976), p. 1-5.

Under the heading "English," this bibliography lists 1 book in press, 1 monograph, 15 articles in print and 1 in press, 1 paper, and 2 projects having to do with Newfoundland English.

702. Knowlton, Keith A. "Words, wit, and a sagacious sailor." Financial Post, 23 Apr. 1977, p. 22.

This review of Funk and Wagnalls Standard College Dictionary: Canadian Edition, ed. Walter S. Avis, q.v., mentions the dictionary's increased Canadian content and cites Avis's definition of a Canadianism. The dictionary's preference for AE spellings over BE spellings is also noted.

703. Lautens, Trevor. "Borse has run its course." Sun (Vancouver), 4 July 1977.

This records 13 expressions used by Canadian children to lay claim to things.

704 McIver, Jack. "What, me literate?" Globe and Mail (Toronto), 13 Feb. 1976, Advertising Supplement, p. 1.

This records 5 pronunciations and 1 grammatical, 1 lexical, 1 semantic, and 6 spelling idiosyncrasies that the author shares with other speakers of CE.

705. Moelart, John. "Watch Your Language." Weekend Magazine, 11 Sept. 1976, p. 22 and 24-25.

The author objects to poor style and spelling in modern CE, exemplifying his criticism by quotations from Canadian sources. (The article prompted comments from Messrs. Stephen Elliott, J. Yanofsky, H.D. Wightman, Brian Alty, and Paul McDowell, published in Weekend Magazine, 23 Oct. 1976, p. 1 and 19.)

*706. Northup, C.S. "A Bibliography of the English and French Languages in America from 1894 to 1900." DN, 2 (1900-1904), 151-78.

Northup lists 5 articles on CE, 4 of which have been annotated in this Bibliography. The fifth, attributed to John de Soyres in Parish Notes, St. John's Church, Saint John, N.B., the editors have been unable to find.

707. O'Donnell, Al. "Words." Daily Gleaner (Fredericton, N.B.), 10 Sept. 1976, p. 7.

This cites some CE pronunciations the author has heard.

708. O'Malley, Martin. "What's in a word? A bit of Canada." Globe and Mail (Toronto), 4 Mar. 1977, p. 31.

This article gives a one-paragraph story including Canadianisms culled from Funk and Wagnalls Standard College Dictionary: Canadian Edition, ed. Walter S. Avis. It then lists and defines these, adding 4 more from the same source.

*709. Paddock, Harold [J.] "Keep Up the Fince." RLS, No. 5 (21 Jan. 1974), p. 22-29.

This gives a phonetic transcription of an 80-line poem in Newfoundland dialect.

*710. Polson, James. "A Linguistic Questionnaire for British Columbia: a Plan for a Postal Survey of Dialectal Variation in B.C., with an Account of Recent Research." M.A. thesis. Univ. of British Columbia, 1969.

This questionnaire contains 110 items (11 illustrated), many accompanied by data about British Columbia dialect from earlier, unpublished surveys. The data give information on the pronouncing of 13 words and 12 contrasting pairs, on 1 morphological item, and on 31 lexical items.

711. Scargill, M.H. _A Short History of Canadian English_. Victoria, B.C.: Sono Nis, 1977.

The first six chapters of this book relate the vocabulary of CE to the early history and circumstances of the country, these being its sources and resources, fishing, the fur trade, the forests, homesteading, and mining. There are chapters on pronunciation, on grammar, and on Canadian English and linguistic change. A bibliography is included.

*712. Scott, S. Osborne. "The Red River Dialect." _Winnipeg Tribune_, 27 Dec. 1937.

The authors could not obtain a copy of this before going to press.

713. Sčur, G.S., and T.I. Kasatkina. "Some Notes on Canadian English." _Kwartalnik Neofilologiczny_, 24:2-3 (1977), 403-08.

This article gives the results of a study of the relative frequency of the synthetic subjunctive (e.g., _that he go_) as opposed to the analytical subjunctive (e.g., _that he should go_). The former is reported to be more common, mainly because of stylistic conditioning. For the study of newspapers, the authors used the _Canadian Tribune_, the _Montreal Star_, and the _Financial Post_.

714. Shortliffe, Margaret. "Faux Pas?" Letter to the editor. _Whig-Standard_ (Kingston, Ont.), 28 Feb. 1977, p. 6.

This objects to calling a politician a _henchman_, on the grounds that the word is pejorative. (An appended Editor's Note cites "the Oxford dictionary" and "Webster" in defence of the newspaper's usage.)

Shortliffe, Margaret. Cont'd.

715. __________. "More on that word 'henchman.'" Letter to the editor. _Whig-Standard_ (Kingston, Ont.), 8 Mar. 1977, p. 7.

Citing the connotative meaning of _henchman_, and quoting _propaganda_ as a parallel, the writer maintains that her original objection to _henchman_ was justified.

716. Stevenson, Roberta C. "The Pronunciation of English in British Columbia: An Analysis of the Responses to the Phonological Section of the Linguistic Survey of B.C.: Postal Questionnaire (PQ 3)." M.A. thesis. Univ. of British Columbia, 1976.

The author used the replies of 368 informants in 3 age groups and of 3 educational levels. Data are given on the pronunciation of 11 individual words and of 10 contrastive pairs, and the data are discussed in terms of distribution of variants, provincial trends, regional variation, and age-related differences. The data are also compared to the data from other surveys. The author tentatively suggests that there are 3 distinct dialect areas in British Columbia.

*717. Stobie, Margaret. "Backgrounds of the Dialect Called Bungi." _Papers Read before the Historical and Scientific Society of Manitoba_, Series III, No. 24 (1967-68), 65-75.

The author claims that the name _Bungi_, earlier _Bungee_, given to a dialect of CE spoken in the Winnipeg area, originates in Ojibwa _panki_ (Cree _pahki_). The dialect originated from the union of two peoples, Gaelic Scots and Cree, both of whom spoke English as a second language only.

718. Thompson, Colleen. "Learning the Language," in _New Brunswick Inside Out_. Ottawa: Waxwing Productions, 1977. p. 21-23.

This lists 25 words, phrases, and definitions, 7 in quasi-phonetic spelling, said to be common in New Brunswick. Some are jocular in intent.

*719. Van Riper, William R. Report of the Committee on Regionalisms and Linguistic Geography. NADS, 5:1 (Feb. 1973), 47-52.

This includes a brief progress report on the SCE.

720. Walker, Doug. "Three new dictionaries." Lethbridge Herald, 18 Dec. 1976, p. 5.

Among the dictionaries reviewed is Funk and Wagnalls Standard College Dictionary: Canadian Edition, ed. Walter S. Avis, q.v. The review mentions the Canadian content and the size of the dictionary and notes that it included 17 out of 24 selected unfamiliar words.

721. Walker, Laurence. "Auditory Discrimination and Non-standard Dialect: a Newfoundland Example." Alberta Journal of Educational Research, 22 (1976), 154-63.

This article describes 12 northeast Newfoundland dialect features which make homophones of pairs of words which are contrastive in general CE. It then shows that this homophony helps to interfere with the dialect speakers' ability to make distinctions between the members of the homophonous pairs, even when they are contrastively presented.

722. Wanamaker, M[urray] G[orham]. "Who Controls Writing Standards?" EngQ, 9:4 (Winter 1976/1977), 45-52.

This article outlines the results of the author's survey of the spelling policies of 332 "city dailies . . . commercial printers and publishers."

*723. Widdowson, J.D.A. "Speech, Sounds and Taperecorded Evidence in the 'Dictionary of Newfoundland English.'" RLS, No. 6 (2 May 1975), p. 18-20.

The author points out that the lack of early printed sources for Newfoundland dialect makes contemporary pronunciation more important for the dictionary of Newfoundland English. He describes the problems that the editors met and the solutions they devised for these problems.

INDEX
OF CO-AUTHORS AND CO-EDITORS
OF WORKS ANNOTATED